# ADVENTURES OF AN INNER CITY KID

## LESSONS LEARNED

JAY M. SMITH

outskirts press

Adventures of an Inner City Kid
Lessons Learned
All Rights Reserved.
Copyright © 2022 Jay M. Smith
v5.0

The opinions expressed in this manuscript are solely the opinions of the author and do not represent the opinions or thoughts of the publisher. The author has represented and warranted full ownership and/or legal right to publish all the materials in this book.

This book may not be reproduced, transmitted, or stored in whole or in part by any means, including graphic, electronic, or mechanical without the express written consent of the publisher except in the case of brief quotations embodied in critical articles and reviews.

Outskirts Press, Inc.
http://www.outskirtspress.com

ISBN: 978-1-9772-4949-4

Cover Photo © 2022 Jay M. Smith. All rights reserved - used with permission.

Outskirts Press and the "OP" logo are trademarks belonging to Outskirts Press, Inc.

PRINTED IN THE UNITED STATES OF AMERICA

# ACKNOWLEDGMENTS

Words cannot express my heartfelt appreciation for my family's encouragement of me to share my story with fellow universal travelers making their way through life's journey, including my wife, Lucia, and daughters Joy and Sonya. Many times, they patiently listened to my stories of people, places, and events. I'd also like to thank James Patterson for his assistance in reviewing my first nervous efforts. Above all, I like to thank Loisa Collins, who took many of my thoughts and helped to clarify many aspects of my life's journey.

# DEDICATION

To Leona Carrie Johnson, also affectionately known as Annie, to Uncle George, and to all caring human beings who provided food, shelter, protection, and unconditional love to children in need of it all.

> *"To laugh often and much, to win the respect of intelligent people and the affection of children, to earn the appreciation of honest critics and endure the betrayal of false friends, to appreciate beauty, to find the best in others, to leave the world a bit better, whether by a healthy child, a garden patch… to know even one life has breathed easier because you have lived. This is to have succeeded!"*
> Ralph Waldo Emerson

# TABLE OF CONTENTS

Introduction ................................................................. i
Annie and Uncle George .......................................... 1
Different From Where I Came From ...................... 10
Just Keep Falling Forward ....................................... 18
Banker, Activism, and Marriage .............................. 25
I Couldn't Say No .................................................... 30
Valenti, Owens, and The Jackson 5 ........................ 33
Small Part of the Universal Fabric .......................... 37
In Search of Myself ................................................. 40
'Nobody Knows My Name' ..................................... 46
Taking Psychological Inventory .............................. 50
Going in the Wrong Direction ................................ 52
Fear, Anxiety, Confusion, Joy, and Sugar Cane ..... 56
From the Caribbean to Canada – An Odyssey ...... 65
In Charge of State Health Licensing ...................... 74
Memphis to Harlem – Another World ................... 79
Off to Atlanta, Georgia ........................................... 82
Atlanta Dreamland .................................................. 88
Strip Club Experience ............................................. 96
Going into Marriage Again ..................................... 99
Coming Back Home .............................................. 104
Going Into Business (1990s) ................................. 106
The Insurance Business ......................................... 110

London, Paris, Zurich, Venice Experience ............................ 114
A Mother's Passing ............................................................ 115
Another Close Call; Bicycle Freefall.................................... 118
Indiana Sand Dunes ........................................................... 121
Philadelphia Story .............................................................. 123
Jamaica Gathering .............................................................. 125
Marriage Life Third Time Around...................................... 126
South Africa ....................................................................... 131
Italy.................................................................................... 132
Spain And Portugal ............................................................ 137
St. Petersburg, Russia, and the Baltic Countries ............. 138
Retirement/ Giving Back.................................................... 140
Phoenix Experience ............................................................ 142
Yoga, Meditation, Awareness .............................................. 144

# INTRODUCTION

I can only say that I wanted to write my cathartic reminiscence of my life that reflects my memoir by quoting the late distinguished educator Dr. Leo Buscaglia, who urged to truly appreciate life, especially through personal relationships, and to remember to celebrate yourself and your humanness with joy and with wonder and with magic. "I will not have anybody playing follow the guru. Because when you start following my way, it will lead you to me, and you will get lost. The only way to follow is your way, because you are something unique and special. Don't miss yourself!"

# ANNIE AND UNCLE GEORGE

In December 1943, the universal breath of life came into the body of an African American baby boy. The birth took place in an upstairs flat in the Indianapolis inner city. The birth came when the baby's father was fighting for his country and trying to survive in the South Pacific during World War II. The newly wedded wife and mother not quite ready for the responsibilities of parenthood was trying to understand her young life.

Their life story began as is the case with many young lovers, with procreation, hopes, and dreams interrupted by war. This is just a life notation of coming and going and a testament of the magnificent universal influence. For those of us who experience the miracle of being born, the trials and tribulations of living, the challenges of learning how to survive and grow are ever present. Some even became curious as to finding out what makes up life's rainbow and what is at the other end and ultimately their purpose for being alive.

After the war, my parents soon divorced to find their own paths. My dad, a returning African American soldier who served as a master sergeant in the Pacific, eager to find his way and wanting to grow, was confronted with the reality of fewer opportunities because of his race. Yet, like many returning African American soldiers, Dad was determined to make a way regardless of the odds. After all, he had survived the war fighting for his country, giving him more confidence with an expectation that America would be more responsive in terms of opportunities for Black veterans.

My second coming as an infant occurred when my mother's aunt, Mrs. Leona Johnson, intervened and took me from my struggling but well-meaning parents, who ultimately divorced. My great Aunt, Annie, as she was affectionately known took me in, mainly so I would not be raised in a home where there was turmoil, uncertainty, and most importantly lack of the love necessary to raise a child. Ironically, I had been born in the flat where Annie and her husband lived. I went to live there with her and her husband, George Johnson, staying with her until Annie's death fifteen years later. She was born in 1898, lived in a common-law marriage to Uncle George, a janitor at the Indianapolis Union Station, a train station that served as my playground until I went to grade school. As far as Annie was concerned, a clean floor was one that was cleaned by hand while on your knees. She cooked, scrubbed floors, and performed housekeeping and ironing for White people. In short, Annie was a domestic and a damn good one. What she lacked in academic education, she was blessed with a high degree of common sense, wisdom, and vigor. Thank God!

Inside Annie and Uncle George's upstairs four-room flat, aka tenement, we shared with our next-door neighbor (Mr. Bill and Ms. Mabel) the same toilet, bathtub, and sink in the hallway area that separated the two apartments. In the connecting hallway leading to the bathroom, we also shared a telephone that hung on the wall. I was washed in a large tin tub from a baby until I was three years old. At night roaches, who also infested our flat, would scatter when a light was turned on. At times they would be found in the bottom of our drinking glasses. There were mice inside our flat, and outside there were large, aggressive rats in the alleys that could attack if confronted. The alley cats and stray dogs were equally aggressive and better off left alone. In the inner-city aggressiveness and kindness coexisted.

Little did I know at that time that Annie and Uncle George were my guardian angels. They gave me a sense of security, and for the first time, I was shown what love felt like. My angels' kindness, love, and respect for others were a shining light. The fact that Annie was a very good cook made her light shine even brighter.

In retrospect my coming of age, the beginning of my journey, began at age five when my parents in my aunt's presence asked me what grade school I wanted to attend. There was a public grade school across the street from the apartment where I was born and lived. All of the neighborhood kids attended the school. For some reason I stated that I would like to go to the Catholic school almost a mile away. Across the street from St. Bridget Catholic School, my father operated a small co-op grocery store, a retail concept that was ahead of its time. I was impressed while observing the nuns with their strange long black dresses and the children as they played on the school grounds. Thus, I became the only kid in my neighborhood who attended a Catholic school. I was teased to no end. The neighborhood kids constantly accused me of always getting more free days from school and of praying to statues, which I denied but could not explain. I felt that I was no longer just one of the boys in the 'hood where toughness and conformity were always the bottom line. By the time I was seven years old, I had the feeling of being alone, fearful, and inadequate. However, I did feel that the love in Annie and Uncle George's house was undeniable and kept me encouraged. Annie's love was also reflected in her cooking. I could hear and feel deep within her common sense when she spoke. I could see Annie and Uncle George's kindness in their interactions with others. She would not hesitate to listen and advise with empathy, but would be the first to correct someone when the situation called for it. Along with her gift of love at my very early age, Annie taught me many lessons regarding common sense, responsibilities, and respect for others. For an example, "Treat others like you want to be treated." "He who is without sin, throw the first stone." "You know the difference between right and wrong." "Stay away from bad company." Thank God I listened. Her words regarding life seem to flow into my every being.

Early in my childhood, my aunt began to send me to the nearby grocery store to buy food and other household goods. She also sent me to select and buy fresh chicken for dinner. I would walk about a half-mile across the railroad tracks to the chicken shack where I would select a live chicken to be killed, neck chopped off, blood drained, feathers plucked after boiling, and wrapped. Going and coming from the chicken shack or grocery story was an adventure in itself. Crossing the railroad tracks necessitated alertness for oncoming freight trains and people with bad intentions; I would clutch the money in my sweating hands, frightened that someone may take what I had away from me. Where I lived, walking outside my immediate neighborhood could be dangerous. I always had to be on guard and ready to run when any sign of perceived threat or danger appeared. In my neighborhood from the time a kid walked out his door, the ability to identify a dangerous situation, the ability to act or react fast while at the same time being able to play games, forced an inner- city child to grow up fast or suffer bad consequences. In the 1940s and 1950s there were switchblades, hook knives, and homemade zip guns. There were no guns to speak of, but a kid had to be ready to fight, bluff, or run fast.

There were Black policemen in the neighborhood, many of whom were tough but fair. You just couldn't mess up, or else. There were also many more White policemen, who could at times be unpredictable as well as mean-spirited. They let you know in no uncertain terms that they were the law; they wouldn't hesitate to arrest you or worse, if they felt that you got out of line. Many times, their insensitivity was on full display, and that was just how it was. No wonder the neighborhood kids had high anxiety with a good dose of fear when the cops came into view or when they heard a police siren.

At the age of nine, I also experienced my first pain of loss. Uncle George died. Again, the fear of being alone engulfed me, because the person who sat me in his lap and read the newspaper to me was no longer present in my life. Viewing his lifeless body, hearing the Baptist preachers give questionable words of comfort, seeing the anguish of others, and going through the entire process of a funeral was overwhelming and scary for me.

Annie, who was a Baptist, took me to church; sometimes twice on Sundays. We walked a mile to and from church, as very few people at that time had cars. People in the inner city either walked to where they were going, caught a bus or at times called a bootleg cab.

From the time I was four years old and until I attended Catholic school full time, Annie in her role as a domestic would take me along with her to the White peoples' houses to clean, do the ironing, and at times prepare food for parties.

Rain or shine, we rode the street cars to where the Whites lived. There I got to see how and where middle-class Whites lived; their nice and orderly homes with flowers, lawns, grass, and trees. The entire environment was in sharp contrast to where we lived. There it was peaceful, no ambulance or police sirens, very little foot traffic, and the air seemed fresh compared to where we lived. The Whites' neighborhoods were safe places for them.

At the Catholic mission elementary school, nuns were White and belonged to the order of Sisters of Providence. When it came to teaching and behavior, the nuns were strict and played no favorites. As expected, I was an altar boy who served the priest during Mass. At that time, altar boys had to respond in Latin to the priest during Mass. I became good at mumbling Latin. I sensed that the nuns' dedication for us to learn was sincere as well as scary. It was obey, learn, or leave. As their expectation for me to learn increased, so did my fears and insecurities. There were many of us who felt that we were not smart enough to meet the nuns' expectations. I could try to dodge their demands, but there was no place to hide. The fear of failure as a human being can be paralyzing. Why did I feel so anxious and alone? It was like standing on quicksand with the probability of going under at any time. For some reason the nuns saw something positive in me that I didn't see in myself. I had the uneasy feeling that they were closely watching me. My eighth-grade teacher told me that I had potential but did not display what I was capable of doing. I felt guilty that I had not met up to her expectations. I wasn't sure what exactly she meant, but it was clear that I had a long way to go.

Life in the inner city with tent church revivals, pimps, prostitutes, angry cops, hustlers, winos, taverns, pool rooms, and people just trying to survive was at times overwhelming, but full of adventure. Yet at the same time, there was a life rhythm to it all. The smell of soul food, especially barbecued ribs, fried chicken, biscuits, bacon, sausages, fried apples, and eggs made the neighborhood seem alive. And then there was the pungent smell of urine in old apartment building hallways and alleys. The very thought of the sights, smells, and sounds of the struggling but determined African American community is memorable in many ways. There was a sense of caring and respect, as most of the people in the 'hood were in the same boat. Before going out to play I was always reminded to be careful.

During my childhood we played kickball, football, baseball, and basketball in the streets. The little grass we saw was crabgrass full of dandelions and weeds. There were no lawns. We did see bees, butterflies, grasshoppers, and lightning bugs. We don't see as many of these bugs today. We witnessed all kinds of humanity in action, both the good and bad, in the inner city. What an education outside the classroom! And it is worth repeating that if you could not think and/or run fast, you had a problem.

We were cautioned very sternly not to run from the police, something I learned the hard way. Several of us were playing in an alley, and for some reason we were approached by the police in their squad car. When one of the borderline bad boys bolted and started running, the rest of us ran as well. I remember the policeman shouting something, but I was too busy running. The next thing I heard was a gun going off and something whizzing past my ear. We scattered in different directions. I ran up the stairs to where I lived. My aunt immediately could tell that something was wrong. I was sweating as well as out of breath and very frightened. I did not tell her that we ran from the cops, especially after she told me never to run. I learned that lesson the hard way.

The first time I earned some money at an early age was to accompany prostitutes when they met their pick-ups, aka johns, who were White males. The cops would rarely stop a streetwalker if she had a child with her. We were paid twenty-five or fifty cents per walk. The prostitutes were nice to us, and we understood that they were working. They always called us "baby." They would talk about their many experiences with the cops and johns and their opinion of men, whom they felt were easy to manipulate. An education!

The stories we heard from the prostitutes' experiences were unnerving. It is unbelievable what people will do to their fellow human beings to meet their animal needs.

At an early age we understood that anger, frustration, as well as compassion could rapidly appear and/or disappear in a matter of seconds.

Our parents, as well as whoever was responsible for our wellbeing, could not watch us all the time. They had to work long hours to provide food, shelter, and clothing.

Racism in the North, regardless how subtle, was alive and well. The practice of racial discrimination was widely practiced in the areas of job, employment, education, and housing. African Americans had to take the lower-end jobs regardless of qualification. To quote some things that I heard frequently, "If you are White, you are all right; if you are Brown stick around; if you are Black stay back." "It is your world; I am just living in it." "The White man is always right." Basically, the name of the game was to pray and do what you had to do to survive or keep a job, because the race card could be played or used against African Americans at any time or anywhere. The White system let us know where we stood. Staying in your place was the rule. "Get an education that they cannot take away from you" was the goal. I heard that saying many times. Thank God I didn't forget what the old folks said.

A year after Uncle George died, we moved out of the downtown inner city to a, for lack of a better word, working-class neighborhood made up of mostly houses that were predominantly African American. Most of the Whites had already fled the neighborhood. In those days, people were careful to define who was poor, upper poor, or questionable middle class. Such classifications one way or the other would surely insult somebody as we saw ourselves in the same boat. For the first time, we lived in a house that had a small bathroom with a shabby add-on shower, which I could barely fit in, and our own telephone (with a party line) that we did not have to share with another family in the hallway. Our house was right next to a gravel alley, which was not a pretty site. There was a small front yard with grass and a maple tree. In our backyard there was an old mulberry tree, a worn-out peach tree, and a grapevine that produced sour green grapes. There was also an old rodent -infested, broken-down chicken coop (a place where chickens lay their eggs). I hated that dark and rundown coop. It was a scary place to enter. In the yards of some of the better homes there were peach, cherry, and apple trees; so, we sneaked into other people's yards and climbed to pick the fruit. Sometimes we'd take it home, where Annie would make delicious pies. One time we threw rocks at and killed a rabbit. Annie prepared the rabbit for a great meal.

In the 1950s many of our family members, friends, and neighbors were from the South, primarily from Kentucky, Mississippi, and Tennessee. Going out fishing and hunting was commonplace. The old people knew how to prepare deer, rabbits, squirrels, fish, and fowl. The preparation and eating fresh fish (catfish, buffalo, blue gill and perch), rabbits, squirrels, deer, and coon was a delicious event. After being taken out to hunt rabbits and squirrels, I grew to hate shooting/killing animals. Later in my life, it came to me that it wasn't in my nature to kill animals, even to eat. And I hated to hear the sound of a shotgun being fired.

Although I was living in a different Black working-class neighborhood, the meals still included catfish, fried chicken, pork chops, cornbread, pork and beans, meatloaf, corn, sweet potatoes, slaw, greens, cow tongue, "chitlins," pig feet, and on occasion, ham, especially at Easter and Christmas. Some of these food items are now called soul food. While the vegetables were healthy, the greasy foods and how they were prepared were not. It was years after graduation from college before I became more aware of the importance of what we eat. I began to understand the difference between foods that were healthy and those that were not which definitely includes fast foods. Beware and be informed!

In my new neighborhood, I was slow to catch on socially. The new kids were riding bicycles, going to dances, wearing better clothes, and being more socially inclined. I heard all kinds of stories as to how to talk to girls and get over. Most of these stories were highly exaggerated. In addition, I did not know the language art of how to bullshit or rap. Boy, was I square, or so it seemed at the time.

Fortunately, there were a couple of Catholic families in the neighborhood that made my social adjustment easier. In my early teens I was a loner and had very little social confidence. I couldn't dance, and I was shy at heart. Sensing that I was not very confident, I stayed in the house more than I should have. Annie told me in no uncertain terms that I had to get out of the house and make friends. She also showed me some dance steps. I was stiff as a board. Having not been around girls in my old neighborhood, I was also very shy and scared of the opposite sex.

In the late 1950s, the first time I saw an expression of racism occurred when a couple of neighborhood guys went to Broad Ripple Park to swim. At that time

Broad Ripple was the largest swimming facilities in the state. As the city bus entered the park, I saw a sign that said, "Niggers and dogs keep out." The sign had been covered over with white paint, but the words were still clearly visible. I had always wondered why the city, regardless of who put it there, didn't have the sign post immediately removed in the first place.

During my last year in grade school, the nuns informed me that if I took on extra book assignments and wrote book reports and studied hard, I might be in line for a high school scholarship. They again told me in no uncertain terms that I had more abilities than I realized. In looking back, I suspect the nuns saw a young African American boy at age fourteen with something to offer inside him wandering in the wilderness and in need of prayer and guidance. There was nothing else they could do. God bless them. The nuns also encouraged me to consider going into the priesthood and offered to recommend me to attend a seminary college. Their suggestion scared me, plus I was not good in languages. Besides, what seminary would want a student who mumbles Latin? The only thought that I had was to keep moving, and the priesthood was not my next stop.

# DIFFERENT FROM WHERE I CAME FROM

With the knowledge that I could be considered for a scholarship, I began to read more assigned books and writing reports to raise my grade level. These academic efforts caused me to become even more socially isolated, as I had to spend more time studying, although I did find time to watch Dick Clark's American Band Stand and The Early Show. From a teenager's point of view, I should have been out there trying to learn how to talk to girls and dance. The thought of talking to girls scared me to death. Anxiety! How do I deal with that challenge? From several sources, I was told that I was a slow reader and learner. I wonder why?

Attending an all-boys Catholic high school saw me continue coming of age, mentally, physically, and educationally. My second obvious blessing came about when I received a four-year scholarship to the school. The scholarship was for a Negro student who showed academic promise and had financial need.

A Catholic Irish American family of a deceased priest provided the scholarship. In retrospect, the circumstances under which I received the scholarship were a blessing. Some would say receiving such a scholarship was lucky; the old folks call it the right hand of God was on me. My classmate who was to have received the scholarship decided to accept another scholarship to attend seminary for study for the priesthood, so I then became the recipient. Because of this blessing and in honor of the donor family, I vowed that I would contribute to support the school's student-assistance fund for the rest of my life. In retrospect this blessing of receiving a full scholarship taught and encouraged me to give, regardless.

Cathedral was an all-boys Catholic high school, and to its credit had students from different ethnic, economic, and social backgrounds. The level of discipline and education was consistently high. We were expected to learn or leave. My anxieties and fears of failure continued to grow. Could I keep up? Was I smart enough? The question as to my actual identity among predominantly White students from rich, poor, and middle-class backgrounds made the overall environment for me surreal and frightening. I could have been a better student. I could have been a better athlete, but I was unknowingly lost in a growing feeling of insecurity and unexplained anger. And then there was the inner voice, which encouraged me to continue with a periodic shot of happiness and a desire to learn. In retrospect I felt the presence of Annie, her warmth and love. The English, mathematics, religion, and French classes as well as organized basketball and track were challenges, especially for an inner-city kid who had only the basic academic and athletic exposure and very little confidence. Besides, what the hell did I know about speaking French or Shakespearean old English when the verbiage of Mother Africa and the inner city lurked deep inside me? In time, however, the Catholic high school education experience, including the discipline it demanded, began to challenge my interest and stimulate my mind. I wanted to learn more about the world and how I fit in its overall scheme of things.

While I was in in high school, my sense of observation seemed to increase, along with the desire to learn. A strange feeling that there were two of me began to emerge. The physical me experienced high school life, where I participated in basketball and track. When I played varsity basketball and ran track, I knew no one in my family would be there to cheer me on. When it came to my parents' attendance to support me, it was minimal. Although I was disappointed and hurt in not being closer to them, I assumed that they loved me, and I just had to suck it up. There was only one time when my dad came to a game. I was riding the bench, nervous that my dad was there, and when I did enter the game, I didn't play well. I was embarrassed at my self-imposed sense of failure. However, the other part of me functioned differently. Something inside continued to encourage me not to give up and that I was okay. At times I saw myself from outside my body, although the anxieties became even more prevalent. I felt alone and confused. The challenges of being an only child! The song by Marvin Gaye, "What's Going On," applied to me in every sense of the word.

It was obvious that western European education and culture was different from where I came from. It was more than reading, writing, and arithmetic. I learned about St. Thomas Aquinas, Aristotle, Plato, Descartes, Socrates, Shakespeare, Keats, Mark Twain, Kipling, who wrote "The White Man's Burden," and other philosophers and theologians. While western European education was interesting, I was an inner-city kid where such teaching and understanding had little value. Where I came from in real life was right outside our door with a big question mark: How do I make it today without something bad happening? In retrospect, this was my first introduction to being invisible in White America. Where is my place in such a White world? Where are the people of color in the history of the United States and world?

Had African Americans both past and present made any contributions or discoveries that would make the world a better place? Who am I? Why was I here? What is my role in the whole scheme of things? Damn! What is going on? As far as I am concerned, my high school years represented me coming into something and going in to something else (a black hole) without Annie's love beside me. I felt uncomfortably good most of the time, but SHIT!

Our neighborhood barber, a Black Muslim, talked often about the plight of the so-called Negros in America. I became aware that I knew very little about Africa and the African American experience in America. During the early 1960s, the civil and human rights struggle was beginning to take center stage in America after Blacks in America had endured years of struggle, abuse, and neglect. I attended a couple of Muslim services. I was inspired to begin learning more about my own culture, the one that I never left but knew little about. During the services, I was not sure why the women dressed in all white sat on one side and the men in their black suits, shirts, and ties sat on the other. What dignity and self-respect they reflected. These men and women were struggling to make something of themselves and their families like most of us, but they showed pride in who they were in White America. What I observed and the reading materials written by African Americans was not in line with what the news media was telling the public. I was excited to hear that the Black Muslims emphasized African Americans being proud of who they are and that they should work to empower themselves and not be dependent on Whites for their lively hood. They must do for self. Get rid of the slave mentality. However, like most organizations, the Black Muslim organization had their internal problems and human weaknesses and were not generally accepted by the Black community.

By that time my father had remarried and started another family. Now I had a sister and brother. Good news! Although I was much older than they, I was very thankful that I was not completely alone anymore.

My natural birth mother had also remarried for the third time. She continued her journey of trying to make sense of her life while trying to be more responsible. Mom was very capable and was able to find good jobs, considering it was during the times of limited opportunities for women, especially for African American women. She did not take mess from anybody and could hold her own at a party or in an argument. At the end of the day, my mother was a very strong woman and quite an observer of life, although she would say little about what she observed. But when she did speak, most of the time her observations were worth hearing. However, Mom did have difficulties in expressing love, except later when it came to her granddaughters. A lesson learned was that mom did play a significant role in my life, but not in the manor that I needed or necessarily wanted. Sometimes what appears to be a negative in life isn't, later reappears as a positive. But as for me at this point in my life, the nurturing skills were left up to Annie.

Later in life I realized that the universal guidance was on target. What I received from Annie, grandmothers, and others was exactly what I needed. Because I experienced emotionally the difficulties of childhood, I dedicated myself to be a better loving and supporting parent. And yes, at times tough love does matter.

This was challenging for me, as I had no parental playbook to learn from. There are no perfect parents. Each day I had to learn how to be a better parent based on the previous day. Just keep loving and learning.

Much later in life, Mom would suffer from dementia and I would take care of her until she passed. Although my mother was one of the sources of my anger, it was also my honor to have taken care of her. We united in love toward the end of her life. Again, it was the inner voices that whispered encouragement during this period of anger, pain, and immense struggle. Alzheimer's is a wicked disease.

At eighteen years of age, I was present when Annie had what appeared to be a stroke. She tried to talk to me, but only mumbled disjointed words. I immediately took her to the hospital where she was diagnosed with a major stroke. I watched her struggle to breathe, talk, and live. Annie died after several days of struggling to live. I, along with my mother, claimed her body, selected the casket, and made funeral arrangements. My world as I knew it came crashing down. It hurt so much, yet I remember Annie's words of wisdom that she shared with me throughout her life. A year prior to Annie's death, she detected that I was angry about life in general. Annie told me, "Michael, I will not always be around." When does one's grieving stop? What happens to the psyche and physical self when one's protector, the source of love and inspiration, passes on? To whom does one turn for that love and guidance when there is pain as a result of death? Who can one trust for reassurance that life has its rewards and we should keep going? Are these questions redundant? I don't think so.

Annie (my angel) got me to the door of early adulthood. It wasn't until many years later that I realized that the Universal God had been with me all along, and I only had to keep going and be true to that mysterious inner voice that influenced me. I believe until my dying day that Annie is my guardian angel and that it was not happenstance that she entered and departed from my life when she did. Her presence is felt to this day. She is still part of my existence, part of my physical, mental, and spiritual growth for the rest of my entire life. I will make every effort to give back the love and support that was given to me. Is it a challenge at times? Yes! But it is that inner voice that continues to compel me through my hills and valleys. I believe that it is our ancestors, the collective universal spirits, who inspire us. Regardless, there is something that is bigger than us that provides guidance as well as energy that motivates our humanity. We as humans are guided toward our purpose for being on earth, if we decide to accept the challenge of living life with love and generosity of spirit. We all have choices to make. It is a climb.

As a shy, skinny kid from the streets, armed with what I had learned from Annie and Catholic education, I tried to focus. How do you even spell focus, let alone put it into practice when fear has blurred your vision? However, I somehow felt that Annie had me to move forward to continue her legacy of love. How does one explain being scared and inspired at the same time? In retrospect, I came to believe later in life that the universe with all its spiritual powers was in ultimate control. I supply only the energy, will, and body. It was slowly becoming apparent that nothing happens until you take some action. The elders used to say nothing ventured nothing gained. My first life survival battle as a growing human being was on.

My father sold my aunt's house with the understanding that the limited net proceeds from the sale would go toward paying for my education; more about that later. After Annie's passing, I moved in with my father, stepmother, and sister. Before leaving for college, I lived with them until I graduated, and married, several months later. I was literally coming and going all at the same time. During the time of living in another house, I was the outsider, feeling alone without love in a house that lacked warmth and had marital struggles. In short, I had the feeling that my stepmother did not want me in her house. The fun part was having my little sister around. My father was constantly on the road due to his job responsibilities. I had the distinct feeling that he felt better while on the road. While Dad was able to get away from helping to provide some form of parental balance, my sister, brother, and I were left to make our own way. Thank God I would be away at college most of the time. Thus, I was again in the presence of a person who did not know how to be a parent. Like my natural birth mother, my stepmother had a difficult time in expressing love, basically not a nurturing kind of person. Damn, a repeat! What is going on? Why me? My stepmother was intelligent, a college graduate, and very tight when it came to dealing with money. She expressed love, but in her own way. My dad left me on my own to deal with the negative home front. In all fairness, neither my father, stepmother, nor I had any other choice in the matter. It was what it was. No one promised me a rose garden, but the emotional pain was ever present.

During the summers of my high school years, I worked at a car wash thanks to my Uncle Sam. Also, I worked as a bus boy clearing off tables and washing dishes at a downtown drugstore restaurant. The next job was janitor work for an insurance agency thanks to Annie's help. Cleaning restrooms is a lesson in humility. I didn't realize how men and women could be so messy with their personal hygiene. Prior to going to college, I worked at a popular German restaurant where I was introduced to German cuisine and where I nearly cut off a finger slicing a loaf of freshly baked bread. The owner was of Syrian Jewish descent and a very sharp businessman and very demanding. What an experience in observing upper-class White people! There was an obvious difference in their demeaner. They seemed to have a high expectation of being served. For the first time, I saw what White Privilege looked like. I had not seen this behavior in the places where Black people dined. When the restaurant closed at night, it was always late at night after we cleaned up and prepared for next day. If I missed the last bus going to downtown for a transfer to another bus, then I had to walk two miles from the restaurant to where I lived. Scary! For a Black man, walking through White neighborhoods late at night was very dangerous. There was the dark of night, walking alone, and then there were the White cops.

Prior to my leaving for college, the owner told me that he wanted to promote me to head busboy, including setting up tables, with a promise that I would be promoted to waiter. It sounded like more work to me. My response was, "Sorry, Mr. T.; I am leaving for college." I never forgot the expression on his face and the pride I felt when I announced that I was going to college. It was one of my first expressions of self-determination and control over my destiny. It felt good.

The summer before my close high school friends and I left for college, we got in some fun times. We played cards, went to parties, and enjoyed the experience of dating our high school sweethearts; good memories. Growing up in the middle 1960s there was the Civil Rights Movement, Angela Davis, Eldridge Cleaver, Nikki Giovanni, Frantz Fanon, James Baldwin, Stokely Carmichael, Bobby Seale, H. Rap Brown, President John Kennedy, Robert Kennedy, Malcom X, and Muhammad Ali. It was the time of enlightenment, drugs, James Brown, Aretha Franklin, Motown, and birth control pills.

# JUST KEEP FALLING FORWARD

The experience of applying to college, being rejected by two schools and accepted by two schools over a period of a couple of months without encouragement from anyone was tough. Basically, it was up to me to negotiate the maze with very little counseling; to find my own way. The anxiety of possible failure came and went and came again.

I had the opportunity to apply at the University of Notre Dame but was thoroughly intimidated and doubted my ability to survive academically or meet the financial requirements. In hindsight I could have competed academically, with the assistance of financial aid, work-study, and summer jobs. I was accepted at Ball State Teachers College and at a small Catholic college in Illinois. Indiana University accepted me on a probationary basis. It took a long time for me to forget why I had been accepted on a probationary basis at Indiana. As it turned out, the school where I was admitted, Ball State University, was the right school for me. Not too big, not too small. I was on my way to college thanks to financial help from my father, a small sum of money from the sale of Annie's house, my savings from part-time work, and funds collected from the insurance company where Annie worked in the cafeteria. Annie was so well thought of by cafeteria workers that the president of the company, cafeteria employees, and its agents collected money to help with my tuition. I received a call from the president's office to come and see him. To my surprise he gave me a check on behalf of all the people who loved Leona Johnson. I'll never forget the kind look on his face. What an honor and blessing!

Once in college, I discovered (I am sure that I was not alone) two bright spots in my life: girls and independence. There were fraternities, sororities, parties, experimentations in human behavior, and of course, the higher-education challenges that demanded my full attention and discipline. However, in another song by Marvin Gaye, I remember the words, Let's Get It On.

The thought of competing with a larger number of better-prepared White students made the academic climb even more challenging. Could I successfully compete and graduate? I was no longer living in a segregated neighborhood of color where there were familiar struggles of everyday life as well as caring. However, there was my inner voice whispering encouragement to go forward. My positive inner voice seemed to battle my anxieties, anger, and fears. In looking back, I am reminded of the saying, "Through the grace of God go I."

I believe that the motivation to go forward was not all of my own doing. There was something else lighting the way and helping me along life's path. As in the case of all human beings, at times I was my own worst enemy. When I had the occasion to make really serious mistakes or cause problems for myself, I was guided away from leaping over the side of a cliff, although there were times when I came very close. I was a life participant, but not necessarily in control. There was the time when I arrived in New York by train after attending a seminar at Harvard. While admiring the bright lights and the overall excitement of being in the big city where I had always wanted to be, I was approached by a prostitute. I was surprised, frightened and curious, when she propositioned me, asking which hotel I was staying in. After entering my room, she began to disrobe while sitting on the other bed facing me. She asked where I was from. As we began to talk, I was confronted with an inner voice asking whether I really wanted to have sex with that fairly attractive woman or what? Within several minutes she was sharing that she was from Texas and told me what got her to New York. We began to talk person to person with me doing most of the listening. After about twenty minutes of talking, she indicated that she had to get back to work. There was a calmness about her after talking. As a matter of fact, I felt with her a certain calmness as well. There I was very conflicted as to what was I doing in the first place. I gave her some money (I don't recall how much), which she accepted and was gone. To this day, I wonder if it was the experience of being around prostitutes as a child that influenced me then. Everything works to the glory of God of the universe.

In most of my college accounting, business, constitutional law, economics, marketing, and statistics classes, I was the only African American student. There was only one other African American student pursuing a business administration degree. The public speaking class was frightening, as I had to speak in front of White students who seemed to be analyzing me from head to toe. In many of those classes I discovered that most of the Whites had never been in the presence of colored people. Isolation can be disruptive when it comes to learning. At the start of my sophomore year, a close neighborhood friend who attended the same Catholic high school where I had graduated enrolled at Ball State. I then had at least one person from my neighborhood whom I knew. He and I remained friends for more than fifty years, until his death.

Just keep falling forward and something good will happen. Toward the end of my sophomore year money was low and my father was forced to get a loan to help pay for my tuition. He also informed me with an apology that he had to use some of Annie's funds from the sale of her house for his family use and vowed to repay it at some point. I told him that it was not necessary, as he was trying to help me financially. However, it was very disappointing to hear that my father took action with Annie's money that was meant for me, but he was trying to do the best he could. However, I felt betrayed. It was another suck-it-up moment.

Like many other students, especially African American males, I had to continuously work to stay in school. The work study program gave me the opportunity to work in the library. What a blessing! I was able to read some of the writings of Descartes, Nietzsche, Freud, and Machiavelli. In some of the classes I was again exposed to Ralph Waldo Emerson, Henry David Thoreau, Eric Hoffer, Rousseau, Mark Twain, and Adam Smith.

I was again exposed to western European learning. There was enlightening information on the Greeks, Rome, English, and French history, but very little about Africa and its ancient civilizations. With the exception of Egypt, Africa and its ancient history was made practically invisible in the educational books I read.

I was a slow reader and not good at writing. Later in adulthood, I learned that I had a form of dyslexia that affected my ability to study. In addition, I experienced mental and physical hunger, a strong feeling of isolation and desperation at the end of my sophomore year. To meet the business administration graduation requirements, I had to take summer classes to make up for classes I had to drop because of work obligations and lack of study time.

Summer school was a lonely experience for me. Most of my friends had left campus. Although I had a work study job as a guide for visiting minority high school students, my funds were very low, and I was hungry. For the first time in my life, I understood what hunger felt like. I remember that Annie had given me three silver dollar coins dated as far back as 1868 that I swore that I would always keep. Unfortunately, the need to have something to eat won out. Because of my lack of knowledge, I used the most valuable coin to purchase a hot dog, potato chips, and soda. The cashier took a long look at the coin, but it didn't matter; I was hungry. Years later I discovered what I had done and was heartbroken, because the coins I spent had significant value. Much later in my life I gave the two remaining silver dollars to my daughters and explained their history.

During that same period, I was again hungry and studying alone in the Student Center. While taking a break, I noticed a billfold. My immediate intention was to turn it in at the receptionist desk. Looking inside the wallet, I saw a five-dollar bill. I had a dilemma to do the right thing and turn in the wallet with the money enclosed or keep the money and get something to eat. Five dollars would last for several days and provide much needed food. With the thought of the Catholic church confessional booth hanging over my religious self and hunger pains, I chose to keep the money. Going to hell could wait. Although I finally left the wallet where I found it minus the five dollars, my conscience bothered me for years for not doing the right thing by taking the wallet with the money inside to the lost and found. I was not a thief, just hungry. I had never before taken something that did not belong to me. Thoughts along those lines later in my adult life left me with a feeling of guilt for my actions so long ago.

Going into my junior year my funds were just about exhausted, so I applied for a full-time job at Chevrolet while taking a full academic load. Crazy! Working an eight-hour second shift at a Chevrolet plant was a blessing in disguise. What a life lesson! I had to run from my last afternoon class and get to the plant to clock in on time. I had to join the union (no choice). All these years later, I still have my UAW (United Auto Workers) union card as a reminder.

The factory employees, Whites and Blacks (most of who were from the South and Appalachia), resented college boys working alongside them. They teased me, complained about anything and everything, and they also joked a lot. One of their jokes went too far. As I was bending over to pick up a gear, one of the White guys goosed me in my butt with the end of a broom handle. He and a few others laughed. Embarrassed and angry, I told him don't ever try that again. After the foreman assigned me to another job and walked away, further instructions from my fellow workers were few and far between. Their thinking was "If you are so smart, you figure it out." There were a couple of times that I was almost seriously injured as a result of not knowing. One time I was taking off auto transmission casings that came from heat treatment without the proper gloves. Without the necessary special gloves, a worker could suffer serious burns to the hands. Fortunately, the foreman saw what was about to occur and came running over to me shouting, "Where are your gloves?" After a couple of close-call situations where I could have been injured, it became clear that while working in the factory, I was no longer a college kid, but a factory worker subject to the rules of the macho men who worked there. At that time there were no women working on the floor. An African American worker and a White Appalachian worker took some interest and began to show me the ropes. In time I was somewhat accepted by the other workers in the section I was in, and as a result, the "college boy" was shown how to become a productive factory worker without getting hassled or injured. However, the workers knew that one day I would get my degree and leave. To this day I still remember some of their faces, how they talked, and what they talked about.

Despite the fact I worked full time, attended classes including summer classes, and tried to keep my grades up, my inner voice continued to encourage me not to give up. Coming home usually after midnight, studying for my morning class and going to bed at three a.m. and sometimes four o'clock in the morning left me tired but more determined. What choice did I have? If I failed my classes, what would I do? Where would I go?

At some point during this period of struggle, I began to feel more confident; however, fear was still very present. There was nourishment or energy that was growing within. I sensed I could survive and get my degree; I just had to keep going. Through the grace of God, I was able to raise my overall grade point to just above a B average in the final eleven months of my college experience. I was also recommended to be admitted to an academic honors society. Admission to the academic honors society would have meant so much to me, my family, my fraternity, and Annie, if I could show how far I had come. Unfortunately, I missed acceptance into the organization by a few points. One more disappointment wasn't going to kill me.

During my senior year, the United States was undergoing civil and human rights struggles. Again, that inner voice encouraged me to get involved. With some apprehension I became involved with a group of like-minded Black and White students regarding the issue of discrimination on-campus and off-campus housing. To my surprise and honor, I was selected president by fellow student members. The integrated group was the first recognized civil rights group on campus. As my activism increased, I decided to join a group to go to Kent State in Ohio to participate in Freedom Rides to the southern states. Prior to my joining the group for the drive to Ohio, my mother called; something she seldom did. I told her I did not have time to talk, as I was on my way to join the Freedom Rides leaving from Ohio. Mother fussed and cussed as well as demanded that I not go. She maintained that I did not know how to turn the other cheek and, in most likelihood, would be killed or put in jail. For whatever reason, my inner voice agreed with her. After trying to resist her demands, a sudden peace came over me. As a matter of history, the Freedom Riders' bus was intercepted somewhere in the South, students were beaten, jailed, and some were even hospitalized. I was mentally hurt and embarrassed for not going on the Freedom Rides. I felt that I had let myself as well as fellow activists down. Again in retrospect, I believe to this day that collective prayers and the universal God interceded. The plan was that I would later serve in another way.

During this period there were the assassinations of Robert F. Kennedy; Dr. Martin Luther King, Jr.; Medgar Evers(NAACP Mississippi field director); Malcolm X (Black Muslims); Fred Hampton ( Black Panther Party); Viola Liuzzo (White female voter-rights activist worker for SNCC); James Chaney, Andrew Goodman, and Michael Schwerner (CORE civil rights workers); the four young Black girls killed in the bombing of 16th Street Baptist Church in Birmingham, Alabama; Jimmie Lee Jackson, a voter rights activist who was beaten and shot by an Alabama state trooper; and many other fellow human beings who were killed because they were of color or stood for justice and equality. It was indeed the best of times and the worst of times. It was a time that "tried men souls."

The Vietnam War was being fought during this period with high casualty rates. Several of my friends were drafted into the armed forces primarily to fight in Vietnam, including childhood friends, as well as some who dropped out of college and were sent to war, but never returned home to their loved ones. While the story of Muhammad Ali, the world heavyweight boxing champion is well documented, Ali was an African American role model. He took a stand against the war, pointing out that "no Vietnamese had done him or his people no harm and that the American government was fighting in an unjust war and should stand up for Black people in America." Ali was ten times the world hero than the American tough-guy actor John Wayne was. A great example of White fantasy versus world reality. There is no doubt as to who is more admired and respected to this day.

# BANKER, ACTIVISM, AND MARRIAGE

After graduating from college and completing several job interviews in South Bend and Logansport, Indiana, I was hired by America Flecther National Bank (AFNB), which is now known as Chase Bank in Indianapolis. The senior vice president of human resources, who was a Catholic, explained that a White trainee and I would be in the bank's first-time management-trainee program that involved spending time in all the major departments. What an experience! As the first African American trainee, a few executive officers, some of them Catholic, took me under their wings. They understood to a degree my precarious situation; that I would be in departments that never had a Black trainee before and a community and civil rights activist. Keep in mind that this took place in the middle and late 1960s during the civil rights protest demonstrations throughout the United States. Although in many of the departments people were pleasant, as they had already been told that I would be coming, I was also greeted with stares, doubtful expressions, and resentment. Older White men IN PARTICULAR seemed the most antagonized. The younger White females seemed more curious and cautiously friendly.

It was my experience in banking that taught me once and for all to walk tall and look people straight in the eye. There were a few funny things that occurred. My fellow trainee, who later became a significant civic leader, and I went to a nearby restaurant where other white-collar executives gathered for lunch. He and I ordered mixed drinks, as was the custom in those days. Having seen martinis being ordered when dining on TV shows, I ordered one, or was it two? On our way back to the bank, it became evident that my head wasn't clear. I spent the rest of the afternoon trying to look busy, seeing double, and praying that no one would come by and smell my breath. What a way to get fired!

The next bank adventure occurred when I was inventorying stacks of new twenty-dollar bills from the Chicago Federal Reserve Bank. Without realizing it at the time, I accidentally knocked over a stack of wrapped twenty-dollar bills into a waste basket. The next morning the manager asked me to come into his office and on his desk was a large stack of new twenty-dollars bills. He told me that the janitor had found the money when he emptied the waste paper basket and asked if I knew how that money happened to end up in the trash basket. For a moment, my heart seemed to stop as I looked on in amazement at the stack of bills still wrapped and tried to figure out how in the hell it happened. After a discussion, he gave me a little smile and told me to go back to work. I felt a strong sense of failure as a bank branch trainee, and I faced the possibility that I could be implicated in breaking the law intentionally or unintentionally, with total embarrassment to my family. I don't remember going home. The entire day was a blank.

At the same branch, I was left in charge when the manager had to attend a meeting. The head teller, an old gruff White woman, and I were left in charge. Just us! A middle-aged man who came into the bank had been obviously drinking and could not clearly write his name on the withdrawal slip to the teller's satisfaction. In addition, the man could not adequately prove his identity. When we informed him that for his own protection and ours, we could not honor his withdrawal slip, the man became loud and frightened the teller, saying that he was going to get his money. After consulting with the head teller, I told her to push the alarm button. Within minutes the police came in with guns drawn. Their action was so swift it frightened the employees and me. The angry man in question seemed to immediately sober up with the display of police with guns drawn. At the same time, my manager came into the bank with a shocked expression on his red face. After everything had calmed down, I explained what occurred and my decision to call the police. He asked to what degree I tried to calm the situation. To this day I appreciate his calmness and the fact that he understood that I was a rookie in a pressure situation with a lot to learn. He could have called personnel and reported the situation as well as have me removed from the bank branch, but he didn't. When I left the bank for good years later, I was told by senior bank officers that I would be welcome back to continue my career in banking. For me, that was the first good news I heard since being hired at the bank.

By that time, I was fully involved in civil rights and social justice in the community. After I became active in the NAACP, it became obvious to me that there was not enough time in a day for a dedicated person to address the wrongs of racism. There were many community meetings that at times were contentious; there were demonstrations and TV and public interviews. Also, I was attending necessary community events where business and community visibility mattered. There were occasional threats from the Klan and constant FBI and local police surveillance. But there were great experiences in working with dedicated men and women, Blacks, Whites, and Jewish community leaders and activists. Most of these civil rights and community leaders were older than me. One such person was Andrew Ramsey, an African American educator, writer, philosopher, and long-time civil rights advocate. Mr. Ramsey was short in statue with a beautiful smile, especially when he shared his thoughts. Mr. Ramsey would talk to our young committed NAACP group in a patient and informative manner. He spoke about understanding how to negotiate, and what to expect when dealing with a racist system, especially in the area of education of African American children. We learned how redlining affects housing for people of color. The practice of redlining on the part of real estate agencies, financial institutions, and local municipalities keeps people of color out of White communities.

Another lesson that I learned from Mr. Ramsey was how based upon a particular issue, to critically think, know your opponent, study the issue to be discussed, and whenever possible have a plan to address a particular issue prior to meeting. This concept took time for me to understand, as my emotions and anxieties at times took control making it difficult to express my complete responses. I had too many thoughts running through my head all at the same time. Eventually I began to slow down my overactive mind, listen, and learn from older and wiser Black men and women as to their experiences, knowledge, and insights. I stand on their shoulders; of that there is no doubt.

## MARRIAGE

After dating for more than two years, my college sweetheart and I made the expected plans to marry. We had a very nice wedding where family and friends came together. It was a joyous time, and I was too young to realize that I was scared to death and not sure of what I was doing. Young and in love, we marched out into the adult world of work. Soon thereafter, another blessing came with the birth of our first child. What a joy!

We were busy as apprentices in our teaching and banking professions. Coming home, living in a three-room apartment, taking care of our baby girl, preparing dinners that were adventures in themselves, there was very little time to get to know each other. We did know that we were working hard to make a better life for ourselves and our growing family.

By the following year I was deeply involved in civil rights and community activities, which consumed a lot more of my time. The hunger to learn, read, and solve the world's problems raged inside me. I understood that as a college graduate it was important to give back to the community. It was something that I never forgot. I also understood that family mattered. Because I was raised Catholic and from a broken home, it was important for me to give my family every advantage and the support that I didn't have as a child.

Oh, the strange beauty of life and the challenges of growing up! The business, community, parenting, and social activities were challenging and fun all at the same time. Thus, there existed a serious growing-up conflict. There were lessons I was learning but did not know I was learning. People were coming and going. Real love, faith, and wisdom are not readily understood when you are a young adult and feeling your Wheaties. Your ego is totally in charge, but there are life's dues to be paid.

Having a job to help support a family notwithstanding, learning how to be a good husband and parent and learning the art of capitalism dominated by White people as well as surviving its pitfalls was an everyday challenge. To move up the business, community, and social ladder, an African American inner-city male had to function successfully in two different cultures; the White majority culture with emphasis on making money, competition, and White privilege and the African American culture, trying to compete for employment, withstand the constant presence of racism based on skin color and hair texture, obtain decent housing and wages, and physically survive. Doing it all at the same time was insane. Basically, the two cultures had different objectives that did not understand each other's methodology, emotions, or definition as to the meaning of the home of the brave and the land of the free. It became obvious early in the game that this economic and social maze had to be mastered without becoming more invisible and suffering a complete loss of identity. Being made a victim because of racism was not an option. I remembered the stories about my father and other African American soldiers coming back to the States from World War II, and again being confronted with racism in housing, employment, and voting rights. The Jim Crow attitude on the part of many Whites and institutions was alive and well, and the police and court system maintained this sacred degree of law and order. As it was then as it is now, where was the justice? Where was the love?

While I was at the bank, the experience I gained in commercial, personal, and small business loan departments as well as branch banking were invaluable later in my life. It gave me the opportunity to inform and help educate other African Americans who were not as aware of how the financial system worked in general. How can one grow and prosper in a system that they do not understand? And how can they make that White economic system work for them and their families? I continued to have the uneasy feeling that I was going from one department to another on clouds with many storm warnings. Fear, joy, and inspiration served as my source of energy and pushed me forward.

# I COULDN'T SAY NO

In 1968, as I entered my third year of banking, I was approached by an African American male who later became one of my mentors, role models, and friend. He was bigger than life with an obvious love for people, a great laugh, and a quick mind. His name was Sylvester Rowe. I began to learn how to relax and focus under his tutelage. He remained a mentor and friend until he passed away years later. God bless him. He believed that I could be of greater service to the community by helping implement a voluntary service program for people who were unemployed. The three-year experimental program was being sponsored by the Chamber of Commerce, a major participant in the growth of the business community, and funded by the National Association of Manufacturers (NAM). NAM, founded in 1895, is one of the most effective and influential advocates for manufacturers and represents 14,000 member businesses and manufacturing companies throughout the United States.

At a Chamber of Commerce request, the bank agreed to give me a leave of absence to help develop and implement the community program that involved training and paring mostly white-collared professionals with identified unemployed minority individuals searching for employment. As a Black person dedicated to civil and human rights, I was excited to take on the challenge. Although my potential career in banking was of importance, I could not turn down the opportunity to be of service. Let the chips fall where they may.

The Voluntary Advisory Corp (VAC) was established in the late 1960s with the objective of combating poverty and unemployment through the efforts of the private sector other than government programs. VAC utilized volunteers drawn from local businesses who were trained to work with unemployed participants. The volunteer would then be matched to form a buddy system with the purpose of teaching the person how to serve as a sounding board in an effort to help with that person's self-confidence and prepare the person for job interviews. The experimental VAC program, with a dedicated staff of only four, was successful and proved that the private and nonprofit sectors could in fact become more involved working in a coordinated manner. I was very proud to be a part of such an innovative program at that time, helping people help themselves and learning more about how businesses worked from a human resource point of view.

After graduation from college, I became part of the White system as a banker, local Chamber of Commerce employee, board member of the inner-city Black YMCA, and member of the Mayor's Community Advisory Committee. What is going on? Did I in fact choose these organizations, or was there something else at work that I wasn't aware of?

Over the next few years, I continued to serve on the Mayor's Advisory Committee, although I felt very uncomfortable; served as officer and board member with the local and state NAACP, the Community Service Council, the Indianapolis Settlement Houses Board, the YMCA local and metropolitan boards, and numerous other nonprofit boards. My prerequisite for serving on a board was that it served the people, especially the Black community. I couldn't say no. On many of these boards I had the privilege of serving with highly respected Black community leaders and my elders. I learned so much from these wise and intelligent men and women on how to negotiate the White system maze. I interacted with Jewish and White people dedicated to advancement of the quality of life in our community. I got to see various community issues from many points of view, which was an eye opener. I considered many of them my life teachers.

I eventually returned to the bank, where I worked in the personnel and small business loan departments. Not long after I returned to the bank, an African American male who had been recently hired as one of the first assistant vice presidents of color asked if I would be interested in assisting in establishing the bank's first minority small business loans operation. One of the primary objectives was to provide financial assistance to minority- and women-owned small businesses. He had faith and inspired me to reach for higher ground. Tom Bolden was a mentor, role model, and became a lifelong friend. Tom moved well and with confidence among his White colleagues, who critically observed him at every meeting. I was beginning to know what a role model looked like functioning within a White financial institution. And I needed one, especially in banking. Although the doors of opportunity were beginning to open for African Americans in corporate America, figuring out how to walk through those doors was another matter.

# VALENTI, OWENS, AND THE JACKSON 5

Beginning in the late 1960s and going forward, the civil rights era was at a critical point, and for me there were happenings that were weird, challenging, and at times very exciting. While attending a Chamber of Commerce business conference luncheon, I sat next to Jack Valenti, former special assistant to the late President Lyndon Johnson and later president of the Motion Picture Association of America (Academy Awards). Mr. Valenti, a very outgoing man with a keen mind and with the confidence of a bull fighter, talked about many subjects and asked me a few questions. I tried the best that I could not to show nervousness in his presence. I remember what Annie and other elders used to say: just be yourself. Prior to the conclusion of the luncheon, Mr. Valenti told me that he thought I would go a long way. He gave me his business card, which I still have to this day, with an invitation to contact him whenever I visit Los Angeles. We all need encouragement. Getting that encouragement from a Jack Valenti was powerful blessing for me.

Not long after receiving a confidence booster from Mr. Valenti, I was contacted by a college friend and fraternity brother who indicated that he wanted to build a country club in my hometown, a place where African Americans could join, play golf, dine, dance, participate in sports activities including swimming, and have meetings. What an opportunity for the African American community to gain a better self-image and enjoy a better quality of life. Membership would be open to whoever was willing to pay the annual dues that were reasonable. The great track star Jesse Owens was among the first to come and speak before club members, as well as congressmen, professional athletes, and entertainers. While our founding board of directors thought such a club would bolster the overall social, political, and economic opportunities for the entire community, especially in the African American community; we failed to realize that the thought of Black people having a country club was beyond many people's imaginations. Although the concept of such a first-class establishment was greeted positively by those who saw its many benefits, there were others who believed that such a club represented elitism. After three plus years, we realized that it was the wrong time for such an endeavor and that the community was not ready to support such a significant leap. As a result, active financial membership never rose to what was necessary to operate and maintain the club. Sometimes getting off the plantation challenges the imagination.

For those of us who saw a great opportunity to advance the quality of life of African Americans in Indianapolis, and that we failed to make that dream come true was a major disappointment for me. What I learned was moving any marginalized group of people does not occur overnight. Communities of color must be nourished over time by people with imagination, faith in what they are trying to achieve, and a willingness to take risks. Apparently our group's dream was ahead of its time.

## JACKSON 5

I give thanks to Joe Jackson, father of The Jackson 5, who consented to have his iconic singing group perform in our city to help raise funds for the upcoming NAACP National Convention. The Jacksons came in several days before the event. First they had a demanding routine. There were tutorial lessons followed by practice, food, and alleged rest. To organize the event, promote it, and set up security and transportation, several young dedicated NAACP men for whom I was a coordinator enthusiastically went to work on accomplishing our tasks. It was interesting being in the same hotel room with Mr. Jackson, the tutor, and the five brothers who were noticeably quiet. For the first time, I noticed that they were just teenagers, all with different personalities, needs, and insecurities. Some of the brothers were sensitive regarding Michael, who was very quiet and receiving most of the attention. I tried to talk to a couple of the brothers, but for the most part they appeared to be shy and disciplined. It appeared that their father controlled every aspect of his children's actions. There was no doubt that their father was in charge. I, along with several of my NAACP coordinators, accompanied the group to practice, and after the sound systems were tested, there was an explosion of energy with the songs and dance steps that the Jackson 5 was known for. I could not believe the transformation these young teenagers made from just sitting around in their hotel rooms to being on stage. The night of their performance was electric. The excited crowd was a mass of energy. The mothers seemed just as excited as their daughters. I prayed that they would not come out of their seats and rush the stage. For those of us who pulled off the event of a lifetime and literally survived trial by fire, we were very proud of what we accomplished. But damn, we were glad that it was over!

In the early 1970s my wife and I had the opportunity to travel to Spain on a discounted group fare thanks to our college alumni association. After four years of marriage and one beautiful baby girl, we were able to have a real vacation. We visited Madrid and Majorca, one of Spain's Balearic Islands in the Mediterranean. It was our first experience out of the United States. I felt good and very laid back. There we came in contact with vacationers from England, France, Germany, and Sweden. My developing intuition was working overtime. The excitement of being with and observing such a diverse group of human beings energized me. I discovered that I could interact with people from different countries and backgrounds with confidence. It felt good. Walking the wide boulevards of Madrid, enjoying art, food, and wine and the fourteenth- and fifteenth-century architecture which was awesome. My imagination was ignited and on fire.

I was disappointed and puzzled by the lack of interest displayed by several close friends when I approached them about joining us on the journey, as it was a great opportunity to visit another country at a reasonable cost. I didn't understand. Why wouldn't someone be at least interested in traveling and seeing part of the world they had never seen before? What was going on?

We enjoyed the entire experience with one major exception, the bullfights. We wanted to see the matadors and bulls and experience the excitement of the fans as it was depicted in the movies. We didn't, however, enjoy watching a bull being worn down in the first twenty minutes after entering the ring by foot-men who encouraged the bull to chase them around the ring and with men on horseback driving lances into the bull's neck. And finally, the matador strutted into the ring with much fanfare, and after waving his red cape in front of the wounded bull a few times, killed the tired, bleeding bull, which really didn't have a fighting chance. As much as we tried, we were the only ones in our section who did not cheer. We felt like we were in the Roman Coliseum thousand years ago watching the gladiators fight to the death. It is a culture thing and we had to respect it. But don't go to a bullfight unless you understand what you are about to see.

We spent the remaining three days in Majorca. It was a beautiful island where the beaches were filled with people enjoying the sun and sea. It was the first time that I observed young and older women topless. For a young Catholic man from a Midwest inner city, it took some getting used to seeing nudity and making mental adjustments. There was no shame on the part of the sunbathers, just enjoyment of what nature had to offer without emotional hang-ups. Why was I so uptight about semi-nudity? Many years later I finally figured it out. My first trip to Spain sparked my dreams and visions of travel to experience the world as it existed and not something that was created in the movies. It was possible that I could go beyond the confines of the inner-city and the limitations of my mind. Possibilities!

# SMALL PART OF THE UNIVERSAL FABRIC

The family years were precious as well as rewarding. Four years after the birth of our first child, we were again blessed with a baby girl. Our baby girl brought much sunshine, beauty, and energy into our household. As time progressed, family and close friends became even more important.

Thanks to my stepmother's mother, we moved into our first house in a nice, diverse, middleclass neighborhood. At last, I saw healthy trees, beautiful flowers, and grass, not crabgrass, just by stepping out the door. There were so many positive activities that were happening. Enjoying Christmas and Thanksgiving, mowing the grass, raking the leaves during the fall, and planting a small garden with my daughters was pure happiness. There were house and card parties and barbecues. The guys played backyard basketball, went to all kinds of clubs, including some that were illegal, for all kinds of reasons. Truly, our guardian angels were watching over us. Out in the streets, we were paying our grown-up dues. Our wives, who were learning to be mothers and wives for the most part, exhibited patience in dealing with their young and well-intentioned husbands. The guys were so busy coming and going with so much energy that our shadows could not keep up. The fun and ignorance of youth!

One of our first neighbors, a fraternity brother who was finishing up his Army service commitment, and I quickly became good friends and cooking buddies. He also introduced me to a young tennis sensation, Arthur Ashe, who was also finishing up his service commitment and who later became an internationally known tennis player, a champion of human rights, and fellow fraternity brother. What a thoughtful, talented, charismatic, and cool human being! We got together at my fraternity brother's house whenever he was in town for a tennis tournament. On one such occasion when he was at my friend's home, Arthur, in a pensive low voice, mentioned recent problems with his heart. It was a sad moment. I remember him saying, "Why did it happen to me?" Arthur Ashe was a person I admire to this day. A great role model! Sadly, Arthur died in the prime of his life. He left a lasting legacy as a tennis icon and activist, but more important, as a human being.

With a college education, as well as determination, our friends were beginning to make their way in their fields of endeavors. Children were being born and we were able to buy newer cars and more modern color televisions and furniture. The sacrifices of our parents and those of our ancestors were beginning to bear fruit. Thanks also to the civil rights struggles and equal opportunity legislations that induced corporations, educational institutions, and other entities to at least consider hiring and/or admitting people of color. We as a whole had to keep fighting for the advancement of people of color and moving up. I say people of color because in America, if you are not White, you are not part of the White membership, and your status is less than that of Whites. Many Whites see themselves as being extraordinary and deserving of any and all benefits of being White. Such belief is called White Supremacy.

Our generations were the first recipients of the new civil rights legislation and opportunities that were fought for by courageous people like Frederick Douglass; W. E. B. Du Bois; Dr. Martin Luther King, Jr.; Medgar Evers; Whitney Young; Fannie Lou Hamer; Shirley Chisholm; Malcom X; Constance Baker Motley; Thurgood Marshall; and many other dedicated Black and White human beings who fought and MANY who laid down their lives for people of color to advance in American society. All of us today stand on these dedicated people's shoulders and owe them a debt that can be repaid only by standing up for the respect and wellbeing of all humankind.

Apart from my daughters, the love for my entire family and close friends was a roller coaster ride at times and a learning experience even to this day. We all are challenged in life as to understanding what love is, how to express love. In life we all experience suffering and pain and try our best to avoid them. At some point in our lives, we come to realize that joy and love of self and humankind is necessary, to reduce our feelings of suffering and pain. Joy and love of self and humankind will provide each of us a sense of purpose and why we were born. Thus, we find ourselves on life's roller coaster of learning what love really is.

Later in life I realized that human beings are a small part of the universal fabric, but we each play an important role in the key of life. Learning universal love requires time, acceptance, effort, and forgiveness, something that doesn't come easy. For me, that internal voice kept repeating that I had to trust God and myself to exit the roller coaster of confusion and find my own way. Okay! The problem was I did not know how to trust or listen at times to that inner voice. Besides, where was that voice coming from? Where is the exit sign to get off this roller coaster? Somebody tell me something!

I did figure out that the more I learned, the more I needed to learn. It seemed an endless road. That voice continued to encourage me to go forward. Where and how, I did not know. Much later in my life I figured out that each individual needs teachers of the physical, mental, and spiritual realm to help us in our quest for self-discovery. It is up to each of us to listen and make choices. That is the way of the world.

# IN SEARCH OF MYSELF

While my intentions were good, the time and distractions of being out in the community and away from my family began to take a toll. The fact that my wife and I married right after college, immediately started a family, and did not take or have the time to get to know each other or ourselves, unfortunately resulted in separation and an unfortunate divorce later followed. Ultimately I had to bear responsibility for the divorce, as I was burning my candle from both ends, which led to all kinds of personal turmoil. My comings and goings proved to be more than I could handle.

Because I had a traditional Catholic background and came from a broken home, the impact of my divorce was devastating. During my childhood, society considered being from a "broken home" not only a stigma but a handicap going forward. It was something to be ashamed of. The church with its negative views toward divorce added to my sense of damnation. I had a tremendous feeling of guilt, anger, and sorrow. However, that inner light was still on, despite my shattered feelings. Separation from my lovely daughters was very painful, beyond words. The only comfort came from that inner reassuring voice.

One occurrence that I will never forget came when I informed my father that my wife and I were getting a divorce. Dad excused himself and went down into the basement and returned with an old wool blanket. He gave it to me and said, "Here, you will need this." What? Although I think I now know what he was getting at, I will never forget his comment and think that was the point.

While I was separated from my wife, a fraternity brother and friend who lived in San Diego after completing his Navy obligation, invited me to come out and spend some time to regroup and get my head together. I had only a momentary hesitation, but that inner voice directed me to go. After my fraternity brother picked me up at the San Diego airport and dropped off my bags at his apartment not far from the beach, he said he wanted to show me something, and we headed for the beach. There we saw the most beautiful sunset going down to what seemed to be level with the ocean. We placed our arms around each other's shoulders in silence and shared that special moment. I felt a deep sense of peace of mind. I think that it was my first time as an adult feeling what being at real peace felt like.

My fraternity brother introduced me to his friends, who were mostly White, which was an experience in itself. They were accepting, noticeably relaxed, and enjoying life. More important for me, I was introduced to people who truly seemed that they cared. They also exposed me to books on higher consciousness. My first exposure to higher consciousness and spiritual-awakening awareness struck me like a bolt of lightning. At most of our visits at friends' apartments, I was offered marijuana, wine, and/or nuts. It became a new and regular occurrence. With these people I witnessed more metaphysical discussions, acceptance, and helping others; just the kind of life exposure I needed at that time.

Going to the beach day or night was inspiring. There is something about water that soothes the spirit. Three friends literally took me to the top of a mountain overlooking San Diego where we smoked a good-sized joint. Afterwards we lifted a wine toast to life and expressed our solidarity by urinating. Why we urinated on the top of the mountain I am not sure, but for whatever the reason, we had good intentions coming from within. For the first time in my life, I felt free to find out who I was or who I was becoming. I was finally beginning to give myself permission to explore the universe without restrictions or permission. Also, the forgiveness of self was important and necessary. The Catholic confessional had become a thing of the past, just another step in confronting the feeling of guilt. More importantly, the people I met in San Diego respected each other's humanity. While they had their life challenges, there was also happiness and joy. It was an experience that I will never forget.

During my stay in San Diego, my fraternity brother suggested that we take a day trip to Tijuana, Mexico, and then travel south along the California Baja peninsula along with his Mexican American girlfriend, a beautiful person inside and out who reminded me of the actress Natalie Wood. The first time in Tijuana was exciting. In the 1970s the city was a place where one could explore, have fun, get in trouble, and drink as much beer and tequila as you wanted. It was suggested that we get away from the tourist areas and go to a local restaurant in the barrio. The only problem was the restaurant was located in a questionable poor neighborhood. While we enjoyed the drinks, delicious home-cooked food, and the locals, a mariachi band came over and played at our table. They played a few songs and then waited to be paid. No problem. We gave them what we thought was a decent tip, but they felt it was not enough. As a matter of fact, their smiles were gone and they looked pissed off. Some of the locals begin to stare at us. Those couple of songs and a safe pathway out of the place cost us a total of twenty dollars.

Once I was back on a main street, it was the first time I was glad to see tourists. Leaving Tijuana, we continued south down the Baja Californian, Mexican peninsula. Beautiful isolated beaches and scenery. We stopped at a small town for a bite to eat and piña colada drinks. While enjoying our drinks and the beautiful surroundings, we observed a White American in his middle twenties who had too much to drink talking back at two Mexican policemen. The policemen beat the drunk American backwards with their billy sticks until he fell into a swimming pool. The Mexican police pulled the guy out of the pool and dragged him away. That sight underscored an important lesson: in another country, don't get drunk, don't get out of control, and don't talk back to the cops. Your constitutional rights and White privilege end when you leave the United States. I must say that most African Americans know better than to talk back to the cops.

Prior to leaving San Diego, I was given a book on higher consciousness, which I kept for years before finally giving it to another pilgrim heading out on their journey. I believe that it was only through the grace of the Universal God that I had those physical, mental-stimulating, and metaphysical experiences. Discussing the meaning and purpose of life with people like me in our thirties encouraged me to look deeper within. What a blessing to have this opportunity during a time of personal confusion and conflict. The Universal God does send angels to assist on our journey, and I believe that I must do the same to help others on their journey. I now believe that it was meant for me to go along this path toward individual enlightenment and stop doubting myself.

Upon my return home, it was difficult to explain my San Diego experience. Anyway, it seemed that no one understood or cared what feelings I was trying to convey. I knew only that fear, anxiety, confusion, and joy were all wrapped up into a bundle that I was trying to make sense of. In retrospect I was going down my own path of struggles as well as opportunities to contribute to the universal plan. My interpretation of contributing to the universe was beginning to take on a more mystical view than that of the material world. Again, I had little knowledge of what was going on. I knew only that there was a change going on within me. I vowed to just keep going.

## ST. THOMAS, VIRGIN ISLANDS

During the time of my marital separation and after my San Diego adventure, a longtime friend and minority health careers colleague invited me to St. Thomas in the Virgin Islands. She was a strong believer in higher consciousness, Chinese astrology, numerology, and non-western religion. In retrospect, she had more insight into me than I had in myself. She gave me space to be alone and encouraged my solitude in search of peace of mind. I had the opportunity to read, walk the beaches, and jog along the hill overlooking Charlotte Amalie Bay and the airport. There was the sun, sea, and nature in all its beauty around me. The more I jogged the more I relaxed. I became aware of another part of me that was not my mind or body. At that time the only thing that I did know was the great feeling I had not experienced before. Outside of citing Catholic prayers, I did not know how to pray or meditate. However, there was an internal calmness that I felt deep within, along with agitation pushing me forward.

One day my friend called and suggested that I go have coffee and listen to some of the local elders who gathered each morning for coffee in a courtyard to discuss current topics and their observations from a third-world perspective. She assured me that I would be well received. What an experience to be greeted by the older wise Black men! I was honored to just sit and listen to their observations and life interpretations. Their wisdom! What a privilege! To this day, I remember their dark dignified faces and discussions.

The island food, the rum, and overall environment each day was a blessed reward. To have the opportunity to experience nature, including iguanas, guava, palm and coconut trees, and beaches. The experiences gave me time, and space for contemplation. For some reason, I was reminded of Henry David Thoreau's thoughts and observation in his book, Walden or Life in *the Woods*.

On one occasion I came across a small green booklet that influenced me for the rest of my life. "The Need for Logic in Religion Among African-Americans" by Sabir Kasib Muhammad. In the Forward, Iman P. El-Amin summarizes the book by stating, "It is not a work for the timid of heart. It is not a work for the fearful mind. It has been written for man and woman of pioneering spirit, ready to brave the challenges to their own ignorance and misconceptions, in order to find the truth and understanding that can bring their lives into a natural order of human productivity and fulfillment. This book may not be for everybody, but it is for everybody who wants to be rightly situated in their God-given mind and role. It is for everyone who truly wants to be himself/herself and have the opportunity to grow himself into his fulfilled potential." The book challenged me to be stronger in going forward in my life's quest. I felt that I was ready to accept that challenge somehow, some way. Time in St. Thomas gave me an opportunity to think, read, and get a better understanding of who I am.

Somewhere there is peace, something beyond what I had learned in the academic, Catholic, Protestant and Islamic environments. It was beyond, but where? And why was I beginning to feel that I was a part of something far beyond myself? I was just beginning to learn how to trust in something that I did not fully understand. And then there was my encouraging mysterious inner voice, a voice that continued coming and going along with the excitement of living, being among friends, and learning more about the female sex. As James Brown, one of my favorite soul singers put it in one of his songs, it is a man's world, but it would be nothing without a woman or a girl. What a crazy world!

I was beginning to realize that I, like all human beings, was paying my physical and mental dues leading to my purpose for being alive; thanks to many people (family, friends, and frenemies) who came into my life. I must admit that it was my women friends who taught me lessons that I would have never learned without them. Wow! ~ I slowly, ever so slowly, began to realize that the gift of free will was a spiritual invitation to become universally whole. Archbishop Desmond Tutu, a Nobel Peace Prize awardee, a moral, and human rights activist expressed in his book, *Made for Goodness,* "But God's call to be perfect is not just a command—it is an invitation. It is an invitation to something possible. It is an invitation to something life-giving, to something joy-creating. God invites us to a godly perfection. Godly perfection is not flawlessness. Godly perfection is wholeness. We learn some of the contours of wholeness from people who fully inhabit their own lives regardless of the circumstances of their lives."

Among all the confusion, anger, frustration, and sorrow going on in my life, there was a reassuring feeling of calmness and going forward as a human being. I will repeat this statement throughout my memoir. My mother used to say, "There is more to come."

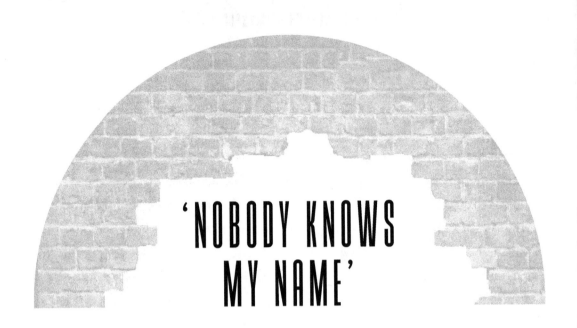

# 'NOBODY KNOWS MY NAME'

Another coming came when I was asked to develop a minority student affairs office and program at Indiana University School of Medicine. What an opportunity and challenge! After I underwent extensive interviews by the dean, senior administrators, and faculty, it was left up to interviews with African American medical students, who had pushed for a creation of a minority office, to determine if I was the right person for the job. For whatever reason, I had a feeling of calmness. I had an internal warm feeling mixed with excitement and confidence. For the first time in my life, I knew that if given the opportunity, I could get the job done as well as help African American men and women obtain medical degrees, thereby helping the community. By that time, I was in my thirties.

During the first few years of my being employed at the medical school, very few White people spoke to me. I was treated as a total stranger and greeted with silent stares. Some health professionals wearing white medical jackets looked away or dropped their heads when we approached each other. Attempts to make people feel invisible can destroy their will to succeed. There were Whites who tried their best to send negative messages. There were only a very few African Americans working in faculty and administrative positions. At that time there were no visible Hispanic or Latinos employed at the mid-level or higher positions. But thank Mother Father God of the Universe for the brothers and sisters of color who were in housekeeping and security. They encouraged and kept me up to date on things that they thought I should know. They knew better than me the kind of position I was in. The Universe provided me with guardian angels and a path.

Annie, my lifelong guardian angel, a woman with a lot of common sense; nuns at the Catholic elementary and high school where the brothers of the Holy Cross emphasized learning and discipline; the opportunities at the bank; mentors who believed in me; community activism that exposed me to people with many interesting agendas and ideas—these blessings of living combined to be the Lights of the World for me to follow a more illuminated path of which I am so grateful. I did not realize at the time that I was mentally as well as spiritually being prepared for the many challenges coming.

At the medical center I was immediately exposed to a different culture, basically White Anglo-Saxon Protestants. One of my challenges on the medical school campus was isolation and learning how to pronounce many of the faculty member's names. There were German, Eastern European, and Jewish names that I had not encountered before or pronounced. For the most part I was treated as a stranger, as portrayed in Ralph Waldo Ellison's book, *Invisible Man*, and in James Baldwin's book, *Nobody Knows My Name*. I contacted my dad to express my anxieties regarding the matter, as no one likes the feeling of rejection. My dad listened and then looked me in the eye without any emotion and said, "It is lonely when you are going up the ladder." Okay! Is that all you have to say? Wow! Where is the love? Then he asked if I wanted another beer. After finishing our beers with a little small talk, we soon went our separate ways with only a goodbye. No embrace. While that coming together and response hurt my feelings, it also encouraged me to be stronger, but a little expression of love would have meant so much. I had a feeling of pain deep within. I felt like I would cry but couldn't get it out.

I was energized by the challenge of learning the medical school culture, protocols, and curriculum. While working with faculty, university administrators, and the community at large I had no choice, if I was to succeed in the recruitment, admission, counseling, and graduation of minority medical students. In the 1970s, there was a nationwide effort to provide minority students more opportunities in higher education and professional schools. Few medical schools sponsored minorities in the health professions seminars. During these early days there were only a few minority-affairs assistant deans and directors. As we became aware of one another's programs, we soon realized that we were the vanguard of such efforts, and we had to increase the number of minority students immediately and effectively. We had to do what we had to do, as the door for opportunities for minorities in professionals could close at any time. Few medical schools sponsored minority students in the health professions seminars. One of the minority student health professions seminars was held at Harvard, which I attended on two occasions. Harvard University was established in 1636 and had graduated several United States presidents such as Barack Obama, W.E.B. Du Bois (First African American to earn a Ph.D. from Harvard), Nobel laureates, and many other major contributors to American culture. Being on the Harvard campus (The Yard), going to a classroom to attend the seminar, going up the steps to the school's famous library, and going over my reading materials there was awesome. Just being there and absorbing the entire atmosphere was awe-inspiring. Although the times at Harvard were not long enough, they propelled my sense of what was possible.

As director of student minority affairs at one of the largest medical schools in the country at that time, I visited other universities and colleges in the state on a regular basis. I advised in general pre-medical students interested in applying to medical schools as well as pre-medical advisors. Periodically I was invited to speak to interested pre-med students at universities outside the state and participate in minority affairs conferences. After I had spent a couple of years involved in minority student affairs, the dean asked me to assume responsibility for expanding the medical school student financial affairs office as the overall student population state wide continued to grow with more students in need of financial assistance as well as counseling. No problem! My banking and personnel experience and business administration degree background was ideal for the new position. I was already working with the University Foundation, Bursar/

Registrar financial service campus-wide office and outside funding sources. All these entities involved a high degree of coordination with regards to medical student tuitions, scholarships, and fellowships. My travel to various medical school satellite campuses increased.

To continue to work on my master's degree, I negotiated with the associate dean of Student Affairs that I would work half days in the summer, take vacation days in the afternoons, and drive one hour to the Indiana University main campus in Bloomington, Indiana, to take the required classes. I would return home between 9:30 and 10:00 p.m. There were a couple of instances when I fell asleep and briefly loss control of my car. I would just roll down the car window, get some fresh air, and keep going.

# TAKING PSYCHOLOGICAL INVENTORY

In order to complete the master's degree, I had a choice to take a human behavior class that required participation as well as evaluation. The course I chose involved a July bicycle trip in hot and humid Florida over a five-day period down route A1A. The purpose of the class and trip was to evaluate response to stressful conditions on a group and individual basis. Our class was divided into small groups. Our subgroup consisted of three females and two males. We could only go as fast as the slowest biker. Being a competitive person, I along with the only other male in our group, immediately broke away from our female companions, who were struggling to keep up. After we agreed to stop for a brief rest, our group had a tense discussion regarding lack of team cooperation and the course purpose. I was embarrassed to realize that I was participating as an individual and not as a member of the bike team, and I made note of that fact in my behavior journal. From that point on our group became closer. With the exception of a couple of days, all groups ate and slept outdoors, preferably close to a church or community center. During the summer, weather in Florida is hot and humid and the air is filled with biting mosquitoes and large bugs I had not seen before. Each day after a small breakfast, we rode from eight a.m. to six p.m. Our group could stop only when all of us agreed to stop for a break, which also caused some frustration and further discussion and compromises. Upon arriving tired and sweaty at our next campsite, we had to write in our individual journals self- and group evaluations based on our class course curriculum. After a day riding in the hot and humid weather, trying to review and analyze behavior is stressful in itself. One observation was that under stressful conditions males and females in the group function as teammates, and sexual interaction was not a concern. At the end of a day, we washed up the best we could; had meals chuck wagon style; participated in our required group discussions, which at times were tense; wrote our evaluations; and immediately went to sleep.

The one beauty of biking was going along route A1A with the Atlantic Ocean within eyesight most of the time. We traveled from St. Augustine through Daytona Beach, Smyrna Beach, Titusville, Cocoa Beach, Melbourne, Vero Beach, Pompano Beach, and Stuart Beach. After completing our bike journey, we stopped at Disney World in Orlando for a well-deserved rest and relaxation. On our long trip back to Indianapolis, the atmosphere was relatively quiet. Our entire group seemed to be reliving their recent life experience and taking psychological inventory of ourselves, which was one of the goals of the behavior class. Although our group did not see each other after our return to Indianapolis, it would be impossible for any of us to forget one another and our Florida bicycle adventure.

# GOING IN THE WRONG DIRECTION

Minority affairs programs nationwide continued to increase numbers of minority professional students and graduates until reverse discrimination lawsuits began to take hold in the late 1970s and severely slowed minority recruitment and admission programs. White conservatives found a new tactic to fight against equal opportunity. They made legal claims that they were victims of reverse discrimination. Efforts toward equal opportunity at the governmental, economic, and academic levels were being altered, and not to the advantage of African Americans. America's experiment with equal opportunity for those who never had it in the first place was being marginalized.

Based on the shortage of physicians throughout the state, especially in the rural areas, the state legislature created a select committee to identify and provide funding for medical students' education in exchange for their commitment to serve in underserved areas within the state. If the committed physicians did not serve in a shortage area, they would be bound to repay the loan.

The dean asked if I would assist him in carrying out the governor's request based on the state mandate. I was to serve as the administrator and financial coordinator who worked with the appointed committee, medical students, and the state in carrying out the recruitment and placement mandate. After a year of carrying multiple responsibilities, my coming-and-going life finally hit the wall.

Off with the superman jersey. With all my other responsibilities, I realized that I could no longer effectively get things done. I was trying to do too many things for too many people. In short, I was losing my identity as well as energy. Not a good thing! Furthermore, why was it that I had been asked to carry such a heavy administrative burden? However well intended the requests from others, I didn't want others to take advantage of me. For the first time in my life, I asked to be relieved of some of my responsibilities, as I no longer could fly like Superman or leap tall buildings. With family concerns, community service, and medical school responsibilities, along with an overinflated ego that was slowly losing air, I was going somewhere, but I didn't know where. A good old ass kicking was in progress. Just what the Universal Doctor ordered!

Although for the most part I had good intentions, I was going in the wrong direction. To respond to all the pressure, I began to party and drink more to reduce my pent-up stress. I must say that I wasn't alone, as other African Americans in various White occupations were feeling similar pressures. I also experienced loss of hair, which was diagnosed as alopecia and I had my first painful gout attack. At times when experiencing a gout attack, I dragged my leg like in the mummy movies. I began to look for love and sex in the wrong places. I had no idea what real love was. How do people learn about the mental and spiritual aspect of meaningful love when they are young, horny, and stressed out? A side note is that I met some beautiful people along the way who like me were searching for life's meaning. I learned a lot from them.

Alone again with no guidance, I was completely on my own, but I wasn't all alone. A male friend became my roommate after we both were divorced about the same time. What an odd couple! A footnote: a number of my friends were going through divorces during the same period. It seemed the more we worked our way up the professional, economic, and social ladder, the greater possibility of divorce increased. Many of us including me, were first-generation college graduates and were not prepared to take on the many demands of joining the White European version of being in the mobile middle class.

There were upsides to moving on up the ladder, and then there were the downsides. In the majority of our situations, we lacked role models to learn from. Most of our parents, neighbors, and relatives, such as my Annie, were working to survive, keep a roof over their heads and food on the table, and more importantly, stay out of trouble with the Man.

The opportunities to keep African American families as well as bodies and souls together have always been a challenge in America. Dr. Martin Luther King, Jr., put it best when he said that one day the Negro will not be judged by the color of his skin, but by the content of his character. Racism can retard and even diminish the human body, mind, and spirit. That is what slavery was all about, for the sake of free labor in order to make money and therefore profit, part of which helped build America. This free labor lasted for more than three hundred plus years. Where was that Christian love and all men are created equal stuff we were taught?

My roommate and I differed in many ways, but we respected each other. We dearly loved our children and were committed to do whatever it took to be active parents and remain financially responsible. We also wanted to have a social life. Therefore we decided that it would be financially feasible for us to become roommates and share living expenses. It was the start of a lifelong friendship. Both of us were from the inner city and understood the ways of the streets and the games people in general played. We were like brothers on a mission to see what life was really about. We allowed each other to be himself. He was from the Chicago projects with a master's degree plus and a commitment to educate children. As fun loving as he was, he cared about people and knew how to be a friend. We had fun and traveled to Atlanta, D.C., Detroit, Las Vegas, St. Louis, Chicago, Louisville, Cincinnati, and Costa Rico. It almost seemed like we were on a mission to do what, I don't know. We made friends along the way. But the most important aspect of our friendship was that we respected and enjoyed people. Our motto: Treat people right, and they will treat you right.

From 1994 to 2014, I heard loud noises in my mind. Confusion! It was like a traffic accident that was always about to happen, and I was the accident victim in the middle of the street. The only question was, when would the accident happen? It was scary as shit. The life path I was going down was sometimes dim, but never dark, yet I was not sure at times if there was a path. Searching for a meaningful life path before sunrise is no fun, especially when there is so much uncertainty. And that may have been the reason why I had so much anxiety and fear.

Interesting experiences continued to happen that contributed to my development and maturity. I went downtown to meet friends at a hotel where a jazz group was playing. Having gotten there early, I found the place packed, as there was a large association meeting in town. As I was about to leave the crowded room, someone motioned me to come over and take a seat. I did, and to my surprise, that person was the famous baseball coach Leo the Lip Durocher and well-known movie and TV actor Peter Graves, best known for his role in the original *Mission Impossible* series and also the brother of James Arness of *Gunsmoke* TV series. Durocher, who was telling Graves a story, asked me what I wanted to drink, which he ordered and continued talking. I do not recall if there were any introductions. At first I was thoroughly intimidated by being in their company and questioned why was I seated at the only available space in the crowded room. What a crazy thought. Both men asked me how I was doing. Graves, whom I was sitting next to, was friendly and periodically acknowledged me. But Leo the Lip Durocher, sitting across from me, seemed to enjoy that he had another person listening to him talk about some of his legendary baseball and personal experiences. Obviously, he loved life and didn't mind telling people about it. I tried to treat it as another person who was at the table. I relaxed, stayed cool, and tried to stay in the moment. I grew from that experience, gained more confidence by sitting at a table among nationally known celebrities I did not know and who did not know me. When I told a few friends of my experience, none of them seemed impressed; neither did they ask any questions about the experience. My feelings were hurt. I couldn't figure out their reactions, and I never mentioned my exciting experience again.

# FEAR, ANXIETY, CONFUSION, JOY, AND SUGAR CANE

Returning to San Diego years later was an adventure in itself. A long-time friend and colleague at the university asked if I would help him move to San Diego. With no hesitation I agreed. When I informed the associate dean of my plans, he looked at me as if I had lost my mind. His question was, "Why are you doing that?" Although I did not directly answer his question as why was I taking the time to travel cross-country with a person he thought was a misfit, I knew that it was a journey I had to take. This is the same associate dean who a year earlier had asked me what I was afraid of. Obviously, he had observed my inner conflict and asked me the question out of nowhere.

On a bright sunny day in October, towing a rental trailer full of furniture, my friend and I set out for San Diego. When the excitement of driving cross-country finally turned into exhaustion, we made our first overnight stop in Oklahoma City. The next day, we were up early and off to our next adventure. While driving through Texas, I saw longhorn cattle for the first time.

We stopped at a diner while still in Texas. Upon entering the small nondescript diner, we were greeted with stares and silence. My friend, who is White with a beard, and both of us wearing shorts and sunglasses apparently surprised the locals wearing worn cowboy hats and jeans. My friend laughed and said, "I'm glad that I am White." As an afterthought, he said, "We are going to die." Actually, we had tasty hamburgers and fries without interruptions. There is something to the thought that at times ignorance and an absence of fear can go a long way.

Somewhere in the mountainous area close to Flagstaff, Arizona, at an altitude of six thousand feet, while admiring the beauty of the mountains and a valley below, my friend lost control of the car as well as the trailer that was pushing the car toward a sharp turn. In short, we were about to go off the side of the mountain. With only about twenty feet to go before our final departure from this life, my friend regained control of the car. We were frozen in time, dumbfounded and amazed at the same time. Being young and macho, we later laughed at our near disaster. It was only years later that we acknowledged how very close we came to dying, and the fear of that thought may have blocked out that frightening experience.

I must say that American landscape is beautiful. My friend and I arrived in Phoenix, where the temperature was 114 degrees, and stopped by a mutual friend's apartment. We said our hellos and immediately jumped into the swimming pool. What a welcome relief! We splashed around like children having not seen a cool pool in a very long time. Damn, it was so hot! After lunch we were again on the road to San Diego. Nearing the city, we begin to smell the ocean and saw beautiful flowers along the highways; a beautiful sight.

Upon arriving at my San Diego friend's new apartment, we unloaded the trailer that nearly got us killed and drank some beer. In the apartment complex there were palms trees and other plants as well as flowers that I had never seen before. After a day's rest, my friend and travel partner and I bade each other a warm farewell. What a cross-country adventure!

Next on the San Diego agenda, I was picked up by my former college classmate and fraternity brother with whom I had spent time during my separation from my wife. Our first stop was Pacific Beach to renew our reunion with

Mother Nature and then on to his apartment. The joy of returning to San Diego and seeing my fraternity brother and his friends again was overwhelming. The following day, I was on my way to the beach and suddenly saw what looked like a familiar face driving by. We saw each other at the same time. Harry, who attended the same Catholic high school where I attended and was my basketball coach in grade school, turned his car around, came alongside me, and called my name. We were in shock as to the random coincidence of meeting each other two thousand miles away from our home state. Was it a coincidence or was it the way it was supposed to be? After somewhat recovering from the shock of meeting in such a way, Harry suggested that we pick up a bottle of wine and go to a nearby beach and then on to his apartment. At the liquor store Harry shared with the clerk our childhood story and sudden meeting. As we were walking along the beach, deep into our conversation, off to the side by some rocks three nice-looking bikini-wearing women were squatting peeing. They thought that we saw them, and they waved to us and with big smiles said, "Hi! We are peeing. What a crazy sight to behold! Harry and I were cool and waved back. What else were we supposed to do? I knew that I was in the right place at the right time. After finding a nice spot to drink our wine, we looked at the ocean and surfers riding the fast-moving waves and renewed our friendship. It was good for both of us to share our thoughts. What a blessing it was.

My fraternity brother and I enjoyed the opportunity to be together again with friends. In the evening, after renewing acquaintances and sharing food, drinks, and laughter, we walked to the nearby beach where the kids were still playing in the ocean. I found that the ocean at night offered energy and awe that only nature provides. Again, I was at a good place with good and caring people, enjoying life.

We heard that the popular singer Bill Withers was to sing in a small setting practically on Del Mar Beach, and tickets were limited. With Bill Withers singing to a small audience and the sound of the ocean in the night with stars all so bright, what else could I have asked for? It was a beautiful experience that I will never forget. An opportunity, yes, but what a blessing at a time when it was most needed.

By the fourth day in San Diego, it was time to again bid farewell and leave for Los Angeles, where I spent a couple of days with another former college mate and fraternity brother. It would take a whole chapter to recount the LA experience. The night clubs, very nice-looking women, impressive restaurants, Venice Beach (no words could explain), and Beverly Hills were fantastic as well as overwhelming for any person. One could easily get lost among the weeds of glamour and the unrealistic lifestyle as to the true nature of what life is or what life is not. But it all looked inviting and at the same time scary.

Next stop was Carmel, California, where I was picked up at the Santa Barbara airport by a longtime friend I had known back in my hometown. What beautiful scenery! The sun, mountains, and flowers all energized me with a sense of wellbeing. I was able to realize a longtime desire to attend the Monterey Jazz Festival, where I saw many of the jazz and blues greats, including John Lee Hooker, Dizzy Gillespie, Stan Getz, and Bonnie Raitt. Wow! The energy of the musicians and audience was off the charts.

While in Carmel I told my friends that I was going to walk down to my favorite bar in downtown Carmel that was owned by movie actor Clint Eastwood. The bar had great ambience and was just a little more than a mile from where I was staying. My friends asked me if I could find it, and I assured them that I could. I was having a nice time talking with the bartender and just relaxing, and the time got away from me. It was getting dark complicated by a thick fog that was rolling in from the ocean. I had to try to beat the aggressive spooky-looking fog. I had no problems with directions for the first several blocks, but then the thick grayish fog caught up with me. The fog seemed alive, right out of a horror movie. From that point, I could see only several feet in front of me. I was disorientated and couldn't tell how far I should go before turning left. It occurred to me that I might be lost because I could not see any familiar landmarks. I had momentary panic. There was no way as a Black man that I was going up to someone's house in Carmel, California in the dark and ask for directions or if I could use their phone. No way! My heart was beating rapidly, eyes were wide open. Suddenly I saw a light post barely visible through the fog. Instinctively I decided to turn left at the light and begin walking north praying that I had made the right decision. Within ten minutes I saw what looked like my friend's white car in the driveway with the house shrouded in fog like in a Hollywood horror movie. As I started to open the gate, I could hardly walk to the door. My fear and anxieties overloaded my body, and froze me where I stood. My heart was in my throat. I could have cried with joy, not sure how in the hell I found the house. When I entered the house totally exhausted, my friends greeted me with concern and relief. I was truly lost and then I was literally found. I have always felt that I was led on a journey through the night dense fog with fear at every step, but I kept going with faith that I would reach where I was going. Lesson learned, never to be forgotten.

Back home again, it was difficult to explain my California experience and the excitement it created in me. It seemed that no one was interested or cared what I was trying to convey. I listened to others, so why wouldn't some interested friends or family members listen to me sometimes? I knew only that fear, anxiety, confusion and joy were all wrapped into a bundle. What was going on in my life?

## TRINIDAD ADVENTURE

A trip to Trinidad led to adventures that would have a profound effect on me later in my life. A group of friends, one from Trinidad, suggested that we travel to Port of Spain for the world-renowned Carnival. It was in Trinidad where I realized that I wasn't as shy as I thought I was and that I had an active imagination. Also, I could be more creative and somewhat comfortable in taking risks. The sense of adventure to try new things and go to new places was real and exciting. Where did that overall feeling come from? I had no previous exposure for doing such things.

As soon as we landed, I had a sense of excitement. It felt good to have arrived in Trinidad. I had no anxieties or fears as to what might happen next. I was looking forward to being in a good place. A Trinidadian friend's mother offered for us to stay at her home and get us costumes to march in one the several Carnival parades. Wow! Again, it was an opportunity to live and experience life from a totally different point of view. It also occurred to me that the cost of travel was not as expensive as I was led to believe, thanks to friends, opportunities, and planning. The more I focused on something, the more confidence I gained. The more I planned, positive things happened, like going to Carnival in Trinidad. After so many years of just going/falling forward, some good came out of going toward a rainbow, and there are many rainbows.

In Trinidad, the diverse people of color, the fantastic soca music, the mixture of African and Indian foods and rum punch stimulated my entire body and imagination. The beautiful people from mixed ethnic backgrounds, women, parties and dancing produced in me happiness and an appreciation for being alive.

The people back home wouldn't believe me when I told them what I experienced in another county. One of our activities took place on an isolated beach where a former army base was located. A new Trinidadian acquaintance was able to gain entrance to a nearby isolated beach, which was a former military base. He and I immediately dove into the blue waters with reckless abandon. We were having so much fun that we failed to notice that a large school of jellyfish had floated toward us and that the ocean tide had begun to come in. Suddenly we were in deeper water. My newfound friend observed with alarm that we were being surrounded by what he thought were dangerous Portuguese man o' war jelly fish. I had noticed them but thought at first that they were floating tennis balls. He told me that we had no choice but to swim laterally and dive deep enough to avoid the jellyfish stingers. Okay! But there was one problem. Back in the Midwest, I had not swum underwater in a swimming pool for more than a few minutes and I was not a good swimmer. There are times when you do what you have to do. A sense of survival, a built-in human gift kicked in. After what seemed like a lifetime of holding my breath, we surfaced and swam the rest of the way to shore, where concerned people had gathered. We were told of the danger that we escaped. It then came to me that I was not only a poor swimmer, but feared swimming in deep water. Sometimes too much excitement and energy without thinking can get one into big trouble, but it sure in the hell was an adventure. Lesson Learned?

Mrs. Romilly, our group housing host was the mother of one of my colleagues at the medical center, and a former Trinidad legislator. She also took in two German women in their twenties who had been unable to find lodging that they thought they had reserved. One of them, Ingrid and I became pen pals for the next fifteen years. Mrs. Romilly, on several occasion while we sat on her front porch shared with me her political, social experiences, and observations about people and politicians in particular. I remain grateful for the wisdom of this no-nonsense, and politically astute woman of apparent African ancestry. I had been given another kind of teacher. Listening and learning.

Each day after an early, delicious breakfast, I would go out and jog in the neighborhood for a couple of miles. At first Mrs. Romilly was concerned about me jogging alone in a neighborhood that I was unfamiliar with. I assured her that I would be safe and there was nothing to be concerned about. Why I was so self-assured, I don't know. While jogging, I saw young men working on their steel pan drums beating the sounds into each section. They were just young Trinidadian men doing their thing for Carnival. Jogging in the Woodbrook section of Port of Spain gave me a sense of belonging. I had no anxieties or fear of not being safe. I saw my people, who were human beings living life the best they could.

Our host took several of us to a sugar cane field to show us what slaves had to deal with. The sugar cane stalks were tall, thick, and intimidating. The minute that I entered the cane field, I immediately felt an uneasy pressure. I was troubled and became serious in thought and quiet. I heard what sounded like frantic screams and undeciphered chaotic noises coming from I didn't know where. That disturbing feeling continued until I exited the cane field. I felt completely exhausted and miserable. Years later, while reading books on the slave trade in the Caribbean, it became painfully clear to me that Europe, especially England, was heavily dependent on sugar, also known as white gold. For hundreds of years Europeans bought, sold, profited from, and enjoyed sugar provided by African slaves free of charge. They helped to perfect the plantation, buying, controlling and selling slaves practices in America. It was part of my journey to be exposed to what my ancestors were subjected to and survived. It comes down to once again Africa, slaves, and profit. A recommended book: *Sugar in the Blood: A Family's Story of Slavery and Empire* by Andrea Stuart.

Only while writing my memoir, I discovered why I was so anxious while in the cane field in Port of Spain, Trinidad. I felt the pain and anguish of slaves who labored under harsh, brutal conditions, many of whom died in those fields. I had walked on hollowed blood-stained ground, and I felt it. I was literally frightened. For more than forty years, when I had brief flashes of the mysterious whaling sounds and the panicked desire to flee from the cane field I could not explain to myself or anyone else what those feelings were or why I had those unsettling feelings. As a matter of fact, I really did not want to talk about the sugar cane field episode.

Now, as I write my remembrances, the Universe also provided flashbacks in my sleep from the first time I was actually on an Indian reservation. I had a similar feeling of suffering at an Indian reservation so long ago. My friend and I were driving to San Diego for the first time, and we decided to see what a real Indian store or trading post looked like on the reservation. We drove miles off the main highway for the experience. I remember the children running around playing, as kids anywhere would. Some of the older and young men stood around with blank expressions on their faces. A few of the younger men briefly looked at us with anger and looked away. My curiosity was replaced with the absorption of the Indian men's sorrow, and fear. As we drove miles back to the main highway, we said very little about our experience, as there was no fun in doing so. It cannot be denied that American Europeans in their efforts to realize Manifest Destiny in America, conquered the Native American Indian and enslaved the African American. To this day there is a large debt that has not been paid. For whatever reason, I was beginning to learn that I was very sensitive to human emotions and could pick up on others' feelings. Who could I turn to about these insights and receive some direction about something I really didn't completely understand?

# FROM THE CARIBBEAN TO CANADA – AN ODYSSEY

One of the Carnival parades started around 2:30 a.m. It went more than a couple of miles with our group part of a troupe in costumes drinking, dancing, and following a band playing calypso and soca music on a flatbed truck. The energy and excitement was unbelievable. The parade ended at sunrise with many participants still dancing. What happiness! In retrospect I can't imagine how all of us danced and partied for several miles and how we got back to where we were staying. The joy of youth is a onetime experience.

After Carnival our group joined another group going to a nearby island of Tobago for a pig roast, rum punch again, music, and dancing. The small island was set up for such activities. There I met two beautiful tall, sun kissed brown-skinned women from Rio de Janeiro, Brazil. They wore large size Hollywood sunglasses, bandanas tied around their heads, and wearing cowboy hats and Rio string bikinis. After line dancing Caribbean style, which was off the hook, we ate grilled barracuda and drank more rum punch. There I was shy and overwhelmed lying on the beach between the two women enjoying the fantasy of communicating with and thanking God for having a beautiful bronze skin woman from Brazil on each side of me. Words cannot describe the happiness. One of the women who could speak limited English took some interest in me, and the entire episode took on more meaning. Between my sexual fantasies and too much rum punch, I fell asleep. By the time I was awakened, the women from Brazil were gone and it was time to leave. The next that I knew, I was back on our boat. The only question I had was where were the two tall women from Brazil with the mind-blowing bikinis and Hollywood sunglasses? I was told that they were on another boat leaving the island a half mile away. That was enough for me. How could I leave such a fantasy of my life without doing something? That something was diving into the ocean and swimming to where my sexual dream of a lifetime awaited my arrival. The minute I went into the water, it came to me that it wasn't a good idea. I began to hear people screaming and pointing at me. A dentist from Wisconsin dove in the water and brought me back to the boat with the aid of a life preserver ring. Back on board, I was embarrassed and somewhat shaken. The captain came over to see if I was okay. With a smile on his face, he informed me that I had dived into the ocean where it was more than one thousand feet deep. I sometimes wonder if the captain had ever seen such foolishness before. The dentist who dove in and came to my rescue and I remained in correspondence for a couple years thereafter. In retrospect he was one of my assigned guardian angels for that trip.

Was there a lesson to be learned? At the time the thought never occurred to me. However, ever since that crazy time, I try to look and listen before I leap into questionable situations. Although I sometimes forget what I learned from some of my misadventures, the image of chasing a bikini fantasy comes back to me. I shake my head, smile, and move on.

Upon our return from Tobago and the rum-punch-party adventure, our cab driver who we contacted to pick us up was waiting to take us back to where we were staying. He was about six feet, three inches in height and well built. He informed us in his Trinidadian accent that we could not ride in his cab, because we were still wet. Apparently I had not fully recovered from my rum party high. I became very angry, cussing while looking for something to fight with. I must say that my behavior was out of character for me, but I snapped. As I went for the cab driver, who was much bigger than me to confront him and get my butt beaten in the process, I was grabbed in a bear hug from behind by a tall, slender dark-skinned brother with Rastafarian dreadlocks down to his waist. He held me firmly by my arm as we walked down the beach and said in a voice similar to that of Bob Marley's that I did not want to fight and that it would do me no good being locked up in a Tobago jail, a bad place to be. Then we stopped, and he asked if I was okay. We walked back to the cab, where everyone was standing still and watching in silence including the dismayed cab driver, who told us to get in the cab. In doing so I turned to thank the brother with the very soft but firm island voice for helping me, but he was gone. He was nowhere in sight. How could anybody disappear so quickly? The wonderment of his immediate intervention, talking to me in such a calm manner, and disappearance will remain with me for the rest of my life with the greatest of gratitude. It was many years later that I realized my Trinidad/Tobago adventures were indeed part of my personal journey with several life and spiritual lessons. In one day I was helped or saved by two human beings, one White and one Black, who came out of nowhere to help a fellow human being who was in the process of making bad decisions. The Light of the World guiding me was my only conclusion, as I had too many close encounters, especially in the Caribbean, that could have gone either way. There is a protective spirit, angels with us, I believe.

While in Port of Spain, Trinidad, I met Gloria the Sophia Loren of my life, while witnessing from the grand stands Carnival's world-famous costume parade. Something immediately came over me, as if I was struck by lightning. I told my group that I would return, and began a journey that would lead me to Toronto, Canada. Eventually I was able to find the section where Gloria was with her family and friends. I politely introduced myself and told her where I was from and where I was staying in Port of Spain. She knew the family where I was staying and introduced me to a few in her party. After an exchange of pleasantries, I was invited to a party the following evening. The next evening Gloria and her beautiful sister and boyfriend picked me up to go to a party, and what a party! We danced to soca music until late into the evening. I usually was not a good dancer, I guess too shy and lacked confidence, however because of my excitement, I caught on to dancing to soca quickly. I met brothers from St. Kitts, St. Bartholomew, and Martinique who seemed interested in this brother from America. They shared their thoughts on island women and what liquor I should not drink, as it might interfere with a man's libido.

I was invited to another party the next night. The delicious Afro/Indian food, the people, and rum punch were enjoyable.

Mrs. Romily was amazed at how quickly I adapted to the people and the environment. She gave me the name of "JJ" from that point of on and would ask about my plans for the next night with a slight smile.

The following day, Gloria asked if I would like to visit her family's home and meet the rest of her family, including her aunt from D.C. What a nice and beautiful family they were! They made me feel at home. I will never forget them.

Leaving Trinidad and the Romilly's home was difficult. It was like leaving part of me in Trinidad. I did learn how to dance to soca music and it was fun.

Gloria, a flight attendant with a velvet British island accent, who lived in Toronto, invited me to visit her. I immediately accepted. Upon my return to Indianapolis from Trinidad, I informed my roommate and mother that I was going to Toronto to visit. For only the second time in my life, I saw my mother look surprised. My roommate had a big smile on his face, but got tired of hearing continuous soca music. After a couple of phone conversations with Gloria, we agreed on a date of arrival and departure. I informed my mother when I was going to drive to Canada. My mother to my surprise expressed concern about the long drive alone and told me that she would pay for round trip airline tickets. Keep in mind that while all the time I was in college, my mother gave me a total of only $200.

Upon my arrival at the Toronto airport, it was good to see Gloria again standing tall with a beautiful smile. Gloria and I spent a fantastic week together going to a play and having dinner with her two friends, a gay flight attendant couple recently returned from Thailand. We also got together with friends, many of whom were from Guyana, South America, and other Caribbean islands. The hospitality, food, and conversations covered a wide range of topics. There was one day that Gloria had to fly. I took the opportunity to walk to Lake Ontario and jog along the lake. Again, I felt freedom and happiness, something that I had not often felt at home. And again, there was the natural elements the sun, sand, and water.

Gloria and I got along very well and had good conversations. We drove over to Niagara Falls, where we had European style lunch and drinks. It was my first time seeing the awesome waterfalls, with their beauty and force of nature. Before I left Toronto, we agreed that she would come to Indianapolis, which she did on two occasions. My friends and immediate family were impressed with her mannerisms, especially her English accent. My mother was impressed, which was pleasant to see. By then I had fallen heads over heels for her, and upon my return to Toronto, I immediately applied for employment at the Bank of Nova Scotia.

In order to live in Canada, it was my understanding at that time, a non-citizen had to be employed by a Canadian company. The bank expressed an interest and requested that I return for an interview. Unfortunately on that occasion there were ice and snow conditions in April. By that time I had been asked to come to Atlanta, Georgia for a job interview. It was sunshine in Atlanta versus winter conditions lasting through April and picking up again in sometime in the fall in Canada.

Although Gloria and I agreed to try and remain in touch, it became obvious that it was almost impossible as time and distance took their toll. The entire experience from Port of Spain to Toronto, Canada was a time that I will never forget. What beautiful people, time, and places. Again, someone came into my life at the right time. Learning lessons of sharing with people life, joy, and happiness. What a beautiful odyssey!

An acquaintance and insurance colleague invited me to join him, his partners, and potential investors to travel to Belize for a possible business opportunity. The opportunity involved construction of a mall and casino. At that time, Belize was a struggling third-world country which had only begun to plan for future development. The business venture depended on which one of the political parties would win the upcoming election. Before sharing my time and adventures in Belize, I must share that throughout my travels in the Caribbean from the late 1970s through the 1980s, the cost was never expensive. Planning and taking advantage of opportunities enabled my exploration.

The Belize business venture included on-site visit to proposed mall locations, presentations by the principals and local politicians, and introductions of all participants, including our potential role in the venture. Our group flew at low altitudes over northern Belize, which was more jungle. It was like being in a movie. My role was to identify and work out details with international insurance resources. I was very anxious and excited to take on such a challenge.

Our meetings and accommodations took place on Belize's largest island, Ambergris Caye. The only significant town on the island was San Pedro. The streets were not paved, for the most part. On weekends the local people would gather on the main street to socialize and dance. What a beautiful sight to be part of! Ten years later, White Americans, Canadians, and Europeans discovered the unspoiled Third World Island and brought with them their version of progress. Now, there is an obvious distinction between the haves and the have nots.

In order to go from Belize City to Ambergris, our group took an open-air water taxi. What a thrill it was, bouncing over sea waves at a good speed as sea water sprayed in my face. I spent four days in conferences, cocktail party on a yacht, tours, and enjoying the local people and the environment.

After boarding the plane for the return trip to Indianapolis, John (now deceased), an attorney and a longtime friend, and I sat back in our seats for takeoff. As the plane gained speed and was about twenty feet off the ground there was a loud bang. There was smoke coming from the right engine. John and I looked at each other with alarm. We knew that it was not a good sound, and then we saw the smoke coming from the engine. The pilot came on the speaker and with a shaky voice said they were having to land because of equipment problems.

Hell, we could see the problem. Once back at the airport, people deplaned in a strange silence. We heard someone saying how lucky we were, since a plane can fly and land with an engine gone, but can't successfully take off with only one of two engines functioning. Thank God it was not our time. It was another reminder that we were spared to contribute at another time and space.

## BARBADOS

While living in Atlanta years later, my second wife and I had the opportunity to go to Barbados, where I outdid myself in stupidity. While leisurely floating in the ocean off the coast of near Bridgetown, I discovered that salt water can keep a person afloat. I relaxed and floated and did not realize that I was being carried out to sea with the outgoing tide. It suddenly occurred to me to look for the beach, which was nowhere in sight. I panicked and momentarily sank underwater. When I surfaced there was nothing but ocean in every direction. As I began to swim toward where I thought the beach was, I became fatigued. Knowing that I could not continue to swim, I thought that if I treaded water and floated periodically, I could survive my precarious situation. What other choice did I have? Ocean salt water gives more buoyancy, thus it allowed me to float for a longer period of time, thank God. Soon I saw the shoreline in the distance and regained some control of my raging fears. When I finally reached shallow water where I could feel the sand underneath my feet, I felt relief and maybe in shock. Later I sat on the beach looking back out at the ocean and considering how far I was away from shore. Years later I finally realized that death was more than a possibility had I been swimming entirely against the tide. I may not have made it to the shore.

During my time in Barbados, I met a White guy from the east coast who was recently released from prison. His wife and mother arranged for a week in Barbados. While we were eating a delicious flying fish sandwich with Barbados yellow hot sauce and drinking the island beer, he shared with me that he went to prison for arson while working for the mob. He invited me to his room, which was at the top of the hotel, for a drink as he continued sharing his misadventures. Off we went, enjoying the island sun, breeze, and our freedom to enjoy life. He wanted to talk about his life experience. Relieved at being out of prison and in Barbados, he began to drink too much rum. The more he talked about how he got involved with the mob, the more he drank. Suddenly, he jumped to his feet, went to the balcony and started to tight-rope walk on the railing. One misstep or a gust of wind would have caused him to fall to his death six stories below. I was surprised at his sudden change in behavior. For him it may have been his first expression of being a free person and enjoying his alcohol high. In a low voice I asked him to get down off the rail.

His response was, "Look, I can do it." After walking several feet on the rail, he got down, still rambling. Shortly after getting down, his wife and mother returned, and seeing the situation apologized and told him it was time to go out to eat. They were both alarmed and embarrassed, while I was trying to figure out what just happened. It was an aw-shit moment. Too much flying fish with island yellow hot sauce and rum made up a crazy combination for two Americans who didn't know any better. Moderation is the best policy.

**San Juan, Puerto Rico**

My Caribbean experience would not be complete without mentioning my brief romance in Puerto Rico. On one occasion I had the opportunity to meet an attractive, intelligent, and charming woman in San Juan. Her style and confidence caught my attention immediately. She took me to places in San Juan that I would never have seen on my own. Having spent time together and upon my return to the island, I couldn't wait to see her again. How in the world did I end up going to local clubs and meeting some of her friends? She spoke better English than I could speak Spanish. Truly, my heart skipped a beat with excitement of it all. The last time that we were in each other's presence, after dinner in a small intimate restaurant looking back across the bay into San Juan, she took me to one of the major hotels where there was a formal dance with a large orchestra playing fantastic Latin music (congas, numerous percussions, and wind and string instruments). We watched from a distance, enjoying vintage Puerto Rican rum. The men wore white formal jackets with black trousers and the women were in various beautiful formal gowns. The entire scene and music were right out of an island movie. I was reminded of Desi Arnaz, who played Ricky Ricardo in the *I Love Lucy* TV series and his Latin band.

On a couple of occasions, she came to Indianapolis on business and I traveled to Puerto Rico. We stayed in touch for a while, but again time and distance placed us on different life paths. Two years later, the Puerto Rican woman, a beautiful human being, married. I was happy for her. How many guys from my old neighborhood(s) could ever dream of having such a real-life experience in the Caribbean?

# IN CHARGE OF STATE HEALTH LICENSING

After ten years of rewarding work at the medical school, I was asked by another governor at that time to develop and implement a legislature-mandated regulatory health professions licensing bureau for the entire state. It was a major undertaking that involved creating a new state agency. Apparently I was recommended for the position; however, prior to appointing me to the position, the governor told me that I had to meet with the Republican Party County chairman as a matter of party protocol. If the chairman had major concerns or objections, the governor would address them. The governor knew that I had voted Democrat on many occasions and suggested that I have a member of his party accompany me to the meeting. I asked my friend and fraternity brother to attend the meeting with me. He was the right person at the right time to be at my side. It was Mother Father of the Universe directing my process through the political system.

Per sunset legislation passed by the state legislature, all health-profession licensing boards would be supported by one administrative department, as opposed to the ten different administrative offices. The bureau would be responsible for licensing, testing, record keeping, and administering state laws regarding all health professionals in the state. The bureau provided administrative services to individual health professional licensing boards appointed by the governor. It was the responsibilities of the boards to regulate and license their professionals per state law. The legislation authorized the governor to appoint an executive director to be responsible for bureau operations and coordination with other state agencies.

Another opportunity.

With the blessing of the dean, I accepted the appointment. I learned later that the governor and the dean of the medical school had already discussed the matter.

A side note: When I was growing up near downtown, we played on a small side street that served as our playground. From there I could see the state Capitol with its large impressive dome. For some reason I felt it was something very special, and for lack of a better description, very familiar. I never lost sight of my vision of the state Capitol, and I didn't know why.

As I stood in the governor's executive office with my dad, his wife, my sister, and supportive aunt via marriage to my uncle, waiting to be sworn in by the governor, I thought about the image of the statehouse that I saw long ago, and now it had become a reality. Unfortunately my mother was not able to attend, another reminder of my grade school days, when my parents were not able to come to PTA meetings. But one person did attend who was very special to me. She was a highly respected superior court judge who had taken me under her wing and encouraged me to step up and step out. A deaf Italian immigrant whose parents brought her to the United States as a child. She overcame her impediments and learned English, in spite of experiencing great difficulty speaking English due to her deafness, and worked on her education. Her story is a testament to humankind and what can be achieved, especially in America. She was my angel, who I have no doubt contributed to my going forward more than I actually knew.

Years later, when I was living in Atlanta, I received a call from her. She informed me that she was dying from cancer and asked me to keep her children in my prayers. I was shocked. What could I say? I don't remember the remainder of the short conversation. I was saddened and honored that she called, considering the fact that we had not spoken since I left Indianapolis. Within several months she died. I still feel her spirit, the sound of her voice, and her words of encouragement. It occurred to me there were a few people who had openly expressed faith in me, most of whom are now deceased. They helped me get to a certain point in life and then they were gone.

Establishing a major department within a state bureaucracy is like climbing Mount Everest. Being given a legislative mandate and being told to make it happen can be both challenging and frightening for anybody, especially for an inner city African American boy raised by a great aunt from the South with only a high school education. I continued to hear a warm inner voice saying, "Everything is okay; keep going."

I assumed licensing, testing, and other regulatory responsibilities for several health-related boards with various regulatory legislative mandates. Among my first responsibilities was to centralize the different boards operations and voluminous records, centralize and change computer programs, and merge staff. I also had to terminate a number of staff members in order to meet legislative budgetary requirements as well as avoid duplication of effort. Terminating a person in general is unpleasant. The terminated staff was all White and mostly middle-aged females, many of whom were the major wage earner in their families and had been employed by their respective boards for years. They were aware of the legislative mandate and were understandably very anxious and angry. Naturally, I was the one who bore the blame for their misfortune.

The entire process was very difficult and at times painful and further complicated by race. I was the young, nonpolitical Black man appointee terminating long-time employed Whites. Of the seventy-five or so staff members, including their bosses, I was the only African American in the building. Even the janitors were White. I had the responsibility of deciding who would be terminated. I could feel the tension as soon as I entered an office. Some employees contacted their legislators, who immediately descended on the governor's office in protest. Ironically, many of these legislators where the same ones who voted in favor of the sunset legislation that created the regulatory agency of which I was the executive director. What had changed?

The governor earned my respect when he invited some of the more powerful legislators into his office with me present to air out their concerns. It was the only time in my young professional life that I felt that I preferred looking older, with some gray hair. It appeared to me that the legislators' thinking was that I was too young to handle such a major responsibility, not White, and probably not intelligent enough. However, they had no choice but to accept the fact that I was a "Negro" sitting in their presence and would be the executive director until I messed up or left the position for any reason. It was a waiting game, and all knew it.

The governor listened to what they had to say, which ironically was very little, and then took a respectful affirmative position, and that was it. He was not going to be pressured. But I understood that the legislators were going to keep a very close eye on me and my department, and if I made one major mistake or slipup of any kind, they would use it as an excuse to get rid of me. In retrospect I felt unusually calm during the meeting. In a way, it was like climbing up Dunn's River Falls in Ocho Rios, Jamaica with slippery footing. If one pays attention as to what they are doing, no problem. But, if one loses focus and slips, then problems may occur.

Although the first several months in the department were very difficult, we were able to work through many of the operational issues and merging of the staff. This was due in large part to a majority of the staff most reluctantly buying into the state's directive and my senior staff efforts. I was blessed with a dedicated administrative assistant from a Hispanic ancestry and a deputy director with Jewish heritage. After a period I began to receive assistance from other key administrators within state government.

It was exciting to be involved in legislative proposals for health licensing legislation. I was beginning to hit my stride, although I knew that I had a long way to go. Appearing and reporting before the various health-related boards was a challenging and nerve-racking experience. On two occasions I had to testify in court as executive director of the health licensing bureau. My writing and verbal skills were noticeably improved.

The everyday challenges as a state health regulator were both demanding and rewarding. The S (Superman) on my chest was growing again. Was it possible I could fly?

One day when I was about to get out of bed and prepare to go to the office, I found that I could not move. After several excruciating minutes of trying to get out of bed, I was able to swing my feet to the floor, but that was all I could do. I tried to raise my arms above my shoulders but could not. I had excruciating pain, experienced panic, and I prayed. For the first time in my life I did not have total control of my body. My body had always responded to whatever physical demand was requested of it.

It took some time before I was able to call my doctor, who prescribed some muscle-relaxing medication. After trying to reach several friends, most of whom had already left for work, I finally was able to reach a friend who could pick up the medication from the pharmacy. The problem was how to get to the door and unlock it. To this day I cannot recall how I got to the door to unlock it. Did I crawl or walk like a mummy? Every movement of my body was painful. According to the doctor, my condition probably was due to stress. Apparently, the inflamed muscles in my back had completely locked up resulting in my immobility. The muscle-relaxer knocked me out for the rest of the day. After twenty-four hours in bed, I began to regain mobility.

When I was able to go to my office, I went with more humility and awareness that body and mind had their limits. Again, I got the point for the need to slow down and gather my nerves. My surging ego was involuntarily slowed down for a short period of time. I still had no idea how to relax. There was too much to do and my ego was still in control.

# MEMPHIS TO HARLEM – ANOTHER WORLD

In the late 1960s my wife and I attended a wedding of a fraternity brother and close friend in Memphis, Tennessee. It was one of our first trips to a southern city, and was it exciting and fun. The southern hospitality and food were something we had not experienced in the North. Partying with my college friends at the Rose Club and eating delicious barbecue, which Memphis was known for, made it all the more memorable. Most importantly, it was how the bride's family received us. It was like being part of the family. I felt that kindness, respect, and love were freely given. Their southern meals and deserts were memorable. Such experiences helped me on my journey and in learning how to treat people. There is no substitute for kindness.

From Memphis, six of us in two cars drove to New York City to continue the marriage celebration. I must admit that in the South driving through the mountains and over roadways in the 1960s was unsettling. Somewhere in the Tennessee mountains in late evening, we stopped at a small roadside diner with the largest Confederate flag on the wall that we had ever seen. For us it was an aw-shit moment. The few redneck customers seemed to be in shock when six Black people entered out of the darkness of night. Although we tried to act cool, we were scared, as it was in the middle of the civil rights struggle. We were served decent bar food. I guess they needed the money.

Upon arriving in New York City, we went to see *Hello Dolly* on Broadway starring Pearl Bailey, Cab Calloway, and an all African American cast. What an experience, seeing for the first time talented all-Black actors and dancers. We needed that affirmation.

My wife and I took the opportunity to visit her aunt, who lived in Harlem for most of her adult life. Our trip to Harlem was an event in itself. We walked in a section of the city mostly occupied by poor African Americans just trying to survive. People sat on steps and chairs in front of their tenement buildings. There were people looking out of their windows, observing whatever they could see. It was like they were waiting for something to happen, seeking fresh air, and hope. As we walked several blocks to see my wife's aunt, we were observed, checked out by the people who knew that we didn't belong in their neighborhood. It is a strange feeling when you are someplace and you know that the people know that you don't belong. Damn! It was one of the few times that I felt uncomfortable among my own people. Yes, there was fear of possibly being accosted or worse, attacked. What a relief to arrive at the nice, clean, and secure apartment where her aunt lived near 135th Street and 5$^{th}$ Avenue. I liked her from the beginning. She offered us alcohol refreshments, which I readily accepted. Having a drink with her registered with me. She was open and direct, New York style, and full of the rich history of Harlem and her family. It is always good to know your family history and from where they came.

In the 1980s I was reminded of the 1960s Harlem when I saw *The Brother from Another Planet,* a film about a Black alien who lands in Harlem and tries to adapt to life on the streets there.

In recent years I returned to Harlem on a couple of occasions. There I found a Harlem renaissance with more diversity. It included young Whites and people from West Africa. There was more energy, restaurants, cleaner streets, and renovations. The Harlem residents definitely showed more pride in being in a place where there is so much Black history, like the Theresa Hotel and Madam

C. J. Walker's mansion, home of Langston Hughes, and famous Black writers, artists, and musicians. There were photographers who took fabulous pictures of Harlem residents such as Duke Ellington, Ella Fitzgerald, Joe Louis, Paul Robeson, Shirley Chisholm, Adam Clayton Powell (Sr. and Jr.), and so many other African Americans who contributed to the richness of American history.

On our first visit to New York, before we returned to Indiana, my fraternity brothers and I decided to have a boys' night out and go to the famous Smalls Paradise nightclub located in Harlem on 125th Street. Smalls was known for its jazz, entertainment, and classy red décor. We were seated close to the stage where a jazz group was playing. Up comes a middle-aged fully built woman, who asked, "Where you boys from?" As I recall, she sat down with us for a while as we were in the process of ordering drinks. I don't know if she was checking us out or what, but I will never forget her and the robustness she brought to our table.

# OFF TO ATLANTA, GEORGIA

My coming and going continued in a positive way. Upon the recommendation of the medical school dean, as well as that of a local physician highly regarded in the community, I was offered and accepted a job in Atlanta to assist in the expansion of a new medical school, Morehouse School of Medicine. What an opportunity as well as a challenge!

The thought of leaving my daughters and family was again painful; there were no other words to describe such feelings. My inner voice of reassurance gave me the confidence to move forward. Informing family and friends that I was leaving home was joyous, sad, and difficult. There was one person that I had to inform of my departure that I dreaded, and that was the governor. He had taken a chance and given me an important opportunity. It was he who stood by me when the political wolves came after me. It was he who acknowledged that things would get rough but continued to encourage me. The governor was not at all happy when I personally told him of my decision. He was surprised to hear of my decision to resign. His first couple of words were cuss words. It took all my courage to hold my ground and keep my voice from trembling. My heart was in my throat, because I felt that in a way, I had let him, of all people, down.

Months later, I received one of the state's highest awards, the Sagamore of the

Wabash and a handwritten note from the governor thanking me for a job well done. To this day I have the letter from the state auditor stating that as a result of an audit, no irregularities were found on my watch. From the very beginning of assuming responsibilities as director of the Health Professions Bureau, I was assisted by Judy and Lori, who came with me from Indiana University School of Medicine to take on the challenge and a dedicated staff who became a team, for the most part. Judy, who is Jewish, and Lori, from a Hispanic American background, were both highly competent and loyal. Lesson learned: that an individual needs others to work toward a common good and purpose to be truly successful. Thank God they watched my back, as there was always the possibility of administrative and political sabotage. Words cannot express my appreciation. I will always stand on their shoulders.

I was living in Atlanta, divorced, feeling my way along, and encountering a different environment. For the first time in my life, I was living outside my home state, and of all places, I was living in the South. Atlanta, Georgia, a place of positive Black empowerment and culture was a blessing. Through the grace of Universal God, my journey led me to a city where nurturing and opportunities for African Americans were evident everywhere. Talented, beautiful people of color were exercising their rights to be creative and free to use their God-given rights and talents to be the best that they could be. There were more opportunities, competition, and pitfalls of all kinds. It reminded me of an old saying that all that glitters is not gold. Be good at what you do. Be kind to others. Be careful.

I was surprised of being called a Yankee. Coming from one of the largest medical schools in the country with a good administrative portfolio was not always an advantage. In the South, I had to prove that I belonged all over again, two-fold. I experienced the human emotions of joy, doubt, and anxiety, but this time I was better prepared. For some unknown reason, I was having fun and being in the moment, as there were social possibilities and potential professional advancements around every corner. There were people to meet, places to go, and delicious southern cooking to enjoy. Probably most of all, there were people who looked like me and who were contributing to their communities. To be more exact, there were businessmen, administrators, academicians, bankers, painters, entertainers, athletes, actors, MD's, Ph.D.'s, poets, and politicians of color, and more importantly, there were everyday folks who worked hard to improve their quality of living as well as others. Their ability and faith in God and community was on full display. It was obvious that I had to prove myself and somehow fit into a new culture, but it was a positive challenge.

Morehouse School of Medicine, at that time one of the newest medical schools in the country, was in the process of transitioning from a two-year school to a four-year school of medicine. The president of the school, Dr. Louis Sullivan, had the burden of raising funds to sustain the school in its expansion. To obtain federal, state, and private funding, it was necessary to meet their fund requirements. He also had to identify and recruit qualified faculty to ensure that all accrediting requirements were met. It was left to a small handful of us on the non-faculty side to make sure the school infrastructure was in place, all state and federal requirements were met, and that it operated effectively. How I was recommended for a position at a school located on one of the most prestigious historically Black campuses in the country is another example of people coming into my life to help me on my journey.

Her first name was Frankie, a White woman in her fifties, who had to walk with braces as a result of polio as a child. Her body was twisted because of the severe impairment of her legs. She was very intelligent with good people skills and well known as a consultant within the higher education community. Frankie's task at Morehouse was to take the lead in recruitment of administrators with experience in medical school administration. This was not an easy task, as medical schools across the country had hired very few African Americans at the administrative level prior to the 1980s. I had met Frankie on three occasions at Association of American Medical Colleges meetings when I was at the medical school in Indianapolis. Apparently she saw something in me that led her to contact me regarding a possible job at Morehouse School of Medicine in Atlanta. Up until that time, she had not seen my résumé, and as far as I knew had not contacted my school for references. That would come later. We had seen each other and interacted only a couple of times at the association meetings. But as Frankie told me much later on, she felt I was the right person for a one-of-a-kind job. What I learned later was that she informed the school founder and president she had found the person that would help lead the school in its expansion efforts.

On a trip to Indianapolis for a foundation meeting, Dr. Louis Sullivan, founder and president of Morehouse School of Medicine, called me and suggested that we meet to discuss possible employment. He was very professional, courteous, dignified, and to the point. Dr. Sullivan told me of the challenges that lay ahead and asked if I believed that I was up to those challenges. I responded that I was interested. On his second visit to the city, he informed me that his office had been in touch with IUSM dean regarding the job offer and that he was prepared to offer me the job subject to final interviews in Atlanta with the executive vice president and vice president of finance and the acting academic dean.

After I accepted the position, Frankie continued to work with me in the development of the student financial affairs office and introduced me to other related administrative responsibilities that I may be asked to address. She was my mentor and angel, encouraged me to look at what kinds of systems were necessary and how to get them operational. Frankie knew that I had to reach beyond myself and be as creative as possible to accomplish the school's goals. Again, a person I did not know came into my life and lifted me up.

After a couple of months, Frankie informed me that she would not be returning to the medical school, as the tasks for which she was hired had been achieved. I was on my own to go into uncharted territory without Frankie's expertise. Her reassuring voice and smile were what I needed to believe in the challenge and myself. Thank you, Frankie.

A few years later I heard that she had passed away.

My job as administrative assistant to the executive vice president was to assist in establishing the school's administrative infrastructure, develop student support services, hire necessary non-faculty administrative personnel, and troubleshooting whenever the need arose.

I was responsible for directing the Program Evaluation Review Technique (PERT). PERT is a visual tool used in project planning that helps the school identify various tasks, set start dates, monitor tasks, monitor progress, and determine if the objective(s) were achieved in a timely manner. PERT reporting was also required by one of the federal agencies as part of its title funding to the school.

My overall job was to get various administrative operations up and running. Because of the uniqueness of my responsibilities, my job was to work myself out of a job. An interesting position to be in, but exciting at the same time to literally work oneself out of a job, as more administrative functions came on line and staff hired. Again, my inner voice was reassuring, as I already had experience in keeping going.

It was agreed that I would work for a minimum of three years to get things up and running. As it turned out, I was employed there for more than ten years, a blessing in itself, as my ex-wife and I shared the cost of my oldest daughter's college education plus, and I paid support for my youngest daughter without missing a support payment. I must admit when my oldest daughter called and told me that one of her scholarships ceased because she received a C grade versus maintaining a B in one of her microbiology courses and that more money was needed to make up the difference, I grew additional white hairs. Wondered where the money would come from? Considering my financial obligations, I had to remain employed at an income level that would provide support for my daughters and my cost of living in Atlanta. But my inner voice assured me that everything would be okay. I must give my first wife credit, as she did not push for increases in support during this period. We were able to work out additional expenditures on an amiable basis. In raising our daughters there was dignity and respect, for which I am grateful.

The organization meetings at the medical school were endless. There were so many tasks to be addressed, per directives from the president and/or executive vice president to do whatever was necessary to get the job done. I was told by the first acting dean, "If a mistake was made in the process of getting a job done, beg for forgiveness and continue on." At the time, I didn't know what to make of his advice. Coming from an Anglo-Saxon-controlled medical school, the comment was not only shocking but also frightening, because of possible reprimand or termination. Basically I was given the opportunity to make mistakes as well as to succeed and keep moving forward. What a psychological relief! I had to represent the school in establishing working relationships within the community and with other universities including Baylor, Emory, and the Atlanta University Center. I will never forget the acting dean and cofounder's advice. Just do it, regardless the consequences. To an extent, that advice freed me to move forward and try not to worry if I was wrong.

On the Atlanta University campus, I had the honor of meeting the late Congresswoman Shirley Chisholm. After an introduction by the president of Spellman College, Congresswoman Chisholm, a small woman in stature with a very strong and commanding voice looked up at me with a piercing straightforward smile and asked, "Young man what are you going to do with your life?" She momentarily waited for a reply.

I don't remember my reply, as I was temporarily stunned by her question. With her intense gaze, she wished my colleague and me well and was gone. That question has stayed with me, though. I needed that question coming from a respected African American woman of Shirley Chisholm's stature. Was meeting the congresswoman at that place and time a coincidence? In looking back at all that has happened in my life, I am grateful that meeting took place.

Another happening occurred while eating at Pascal's Restaurant, where Dr. Martin Luther King, Jr., and many other civil rights and political leaders dined and had meetings. Sitting behind us at another table was well known African American poet and activist Maya Angelou. She was eating fried chicken, sweet potatoes, and collard greens, for which Pascal's was well known. Dr. Angelou nodded to us but gave us a stern look, indicating that we should not even think about coming over while she was eating and enjoying her food. Needless to say, we acknowledged her non-verbal communication. Nevertheless, the mere presence of Dr. Maya Angelo was inspirational. It was an honor just to be in her presence and receive her acknowledgement.

# ATLANTA DREAMLAND

Two years later, the medical school's executive vice president asked me to assume responsibilities for the medical school personnel office to expand its functions as a human resources office to serve the needs of the growing institution. Another challenge, but doable. While I worked on the school's retirement program, an opportunity arose for me to attend a seminar sponsored by a major investment insurance company regarding the economy and its potential impact on retirement programs. In the meeting room a small group of administrators heard from Dr. Andrew Brimmer, a Federal Reserve Bank member and a nationally renowned economist. I was aware of Mr. Brimmer, a well-respected African American economist, from my time when I was a business administration major in college and worked in banking. Now I had the honor to be in the same room and listen to him. Also among the participants was Dr. Clifton R. Wharton, Jr., former president of Michigan State University and United States deputy secretary of state. During the break I was able to speak with both distinguished African American men individually. What an honor! If they only knew how it affected me that they took the time to share their thoughts. They served as role models for me and others who were struggling to find their way in a White no-man's land and make a difference.

I had the privilege of meeting my boyhood hero the late Henry (Hank)

Aaron, longtime Hall of Fame baseball star and a good human being. When I was a youngster, I saw Hank play for the Indianapolis Clowns in the Negro Baseball League. During my first year in Atlanta, I attended an NAACP branch meeting at Pascal's, where many civil rights meetings were held. Visitors at the meeting were asked to stand and introduce themselves. After introductions, someone tapped me on my shoulder. It was Henry Louis Aaron, baseball hall of famer. He asked that I join the committee of which he was a member. At that table were several community leaders. I offered and it was agreed to have our next meeting at the medical school.

After the meeting at the school, Mr. Aaron, on his way out the door turned and said, "We (Black people) have a long way to go, and not to let up." We met a couple of more times over the years. He always had a gentle and serious smile. Both Hank and his wife were always a joy to see. Their dignity and strength of character were an inspiration. Black giant!

As a child of the 1950s and 1960s, I followed with passion the careers of Jackie Robinson, Willie Mays, Frank Robinson, Roberto Clemente, Ernie Banks, and other African American baseball players who finally were able to play in the major leagues as of a result of Jackie's athletic abilities, sacrifice, and dedication to making a difference for people of color. I had the incredible experience and will never forget seeing those honorable Black giants play through the emergence of television. America needed to see not only these men's athletic abilities, but also the way they carried themselves. Character and demonstrated abilities win in the long run, regardless the occupation. It seemed like I had been carried on a magical carpet to Atlanta.

Within a short period of time, I was asked to assume responsibilities for the school's second building as well as the lead administrator for development of the school computer system. A sense of fun, fear, and excitement came rushing over my conscientious mind. Am I really in Atlanta, Georgia, at Morehouse School of Medicine? Wow! Is this a reality or dream? My inner voice interceded to calm me down and reminded me that years prior, while I was in Atlanta for an interview, I met another African American hero and leader. It was Dr. Benjamin E. Mays, the imminent former Morehouse College president, professor and mentor to many African American leaders, including Dr. Martin Luther King, Jr.; Dr. Louis Sullivan; Maynard Jackson; Michael Babatunde Olatunji; Julian Bond; and too many other African American men to mention. Dr. Mays's dignity, intellect, and pride of who he was at that place in time filled the air with inspiration. I was invited to join Dr. Mays and a couple of community leaders by a person I knew through the NAACP. Their discussion centered on convincing Dr. Mays to run for a major Atlanta board position. Just being in Dr. Mays's presence and listening to other African American men discussing the need to make a difference in their community was awesome. Although Dr. Mays was older, his strength of character, intelligence, and dignity were evident. To me he was a Black giant!

Sometime, during my first year at Morehouse School of Medicine, I received a call from Dr. Sullivan's wife inviting me and another colleague who recently joined the school faculty to dinner at their home. The other guest was Babatunde Olatunji, a classmate of Dr. Sullivan's at Morehouse. Olatunji (Tunji) has been hailed as the father of African drumming in the United States. Born in Nigeria, Olatunji went on to become an internationally known educator and entertainer for his knowledge in African drumming and history of voodoo. Prior to Olatunji introducing African music and dance in the early 1950s, America knew very little of the rhythms, songs, and dances of Africa. His first album in America, *Drums of Passion*, sold millions of copies. In researching Baba Olatunji's life, I came across a couple of his observations; the *I Love Lucy* television show, Tunji observed that Ricky Ricardo music, "Baba loo, aiy," has its origin from the Africa Yoruba people.

At dinner, Tunji shared one of his often sayings, if you give love, it will come back to you. It may not be from the source you expected, but it will come to you. Obviously, Tunji enjoyed talking and after making a comment or observation, it would be followed with a joyous smile. I will remember Babatunde Olatunji's smile, kind eyes, and his quick wit. He was intelligent, fun to be around, and a teacher. Black giant!

On several occasions I had the opportunity to meet former mayors Maynard Jackson, Andrew Young, and Bill Campbell. And then, there was Julian Bond, who enjoyed teasing me whenever we met each other. Julian, intelligent and with a great sense of humor, a graduate of Morehouse College, was a civil rights activist who served in the Georgia House of Representatives and later became board chairman of the National Association for the Advancement of Colored People (NAACP). Julian followed in the footsteps of Roy Wilkins, who was a prominent national activist in the civil rights movement and longtime executive director of the NAACP.

Several years prior to departing Indianapolis, as president of the local branch of the NAACP, I interacted with Mr. Wilkins regarding funds our local branch had raised thanks to the Jackson 5 show. I must give Joe Jackson credit for agreeing to his sons to perform at the show with money going to our branch in preparation for having a national NAACP convention in our city. Mr. Wilkins, executive director of the national NAACP, a man who interacts with prominent leaders in the civil rights movement across the country, informed me that all funds raised first must be channeled through the national office. He was complimentary about our branch activism, but in a calm and firm voice, Mr. Wilkins told me there were no negotiations to be had. I argued that the local branch raised the money for the national convention and that the majority of the funds should remain in Indianapolis. I tried to hold my own with an African American national leader who consulted with American presidents, corporate CEOs, and the likes of Dr. Martin Luther King, Jr.; Whitney Young; and A. Phillip Randolph. Mr. Wilkins had a very shrewd and cool style. Although I lost the discussion and gave up a large check, I gained more insight and confidence. At least I had my say.

Atlanta, Georgia, was a diverse southern city, a place of opportunity for those who dared to grow outside the box. It gave me the time and opportunity to grow in confidence and self-identification. African Americans were visible and no longer in America's shadows. I saw the reality of walking tall. What a great feeling!

Many notable educators, intellectuals, celebrities, politicians, poets, and civil and human rights leaders, both Black and White, came to the Atlanta University Center. There was Dr. Linus C. Pauling, a two-time Nobel Prize recipient. Dr.

Pauling was awarded two Nobel Prizes, one in chemistry and the other a peace prize. He was a world-renowned scientist and humanitarian. In the mid-1980s, I was invited to attend Dr. Pauling's lecture on the Atlanta University campus. After the informative lecture, which was well attended, I was among five other university members who had dinner with Dr. Pauling at a well-known Atlanta restaurant in Buckhead. Why I was invited to go to dinner and ended up sitting next to such a great international scientist, as well as a man recognized by the world as an advocate for world peace, I didn't know. Dr. Pauling shared his thoughts in an open and caring manner. It was a great life moment for me to hear him and feel the energy and wisdom that was coming from him. The owner of the restaurant recognized Dr. Pauling and sent a waiter over to see if he could visit the table. I informed Dr. Pauling of the request. In a very cordial manner, he invited the owner over. The owner introduced himself and they briefly talked. He seemed to be completely overwhelmed and sat at the table for a time just listening before excusing himself. I was happy for the owner, who seemed overjoyed. I don't remember our party receiving a dinner bill.

Years later I recalled other important opportunities that presented themselves and influenced my life. In the 1970s while sitting in an Indiana University School of Medicine medical student lecture, I listened to the renowned Dr. Elisabeth Kubler-Ross lecture on death and dying; the five common stages of grief: denial, anger, bargaining, depression, and acceptance. Dr. Elisabeth Kubler-Ross was a Swiss-born psychiatrist, a pioneer in death and dying studies. What a fascinating and strange feeling listening as well as thinking about the mysteries of life, death, and dying. How did an African American inner-city kid raised by a great aunt (my first angel) find himself listening to a lecture on dying and death by an internationally known psychiatrist? Years later I came across notes taken at Dr. Kubler-Ross's lecture, she suggested there are no mistakes, no coincidences. All events are blessings given to us to learn from.

In retrospect I was where I was supposed to be, listening and learning regarding the physical and mental aspect of life and death. For the first time in my life, my fear of death and dying began to take on a more in-depth meaning. The quiet whisper inside me was to keep going. Life can be enjoyed and try not to look back.

I met internationally known jazzman Lionel Hampton through mutual family friends on a few occasions in Indianapolis. Lionel always made sure to stop by whenever he was in town or nearby to have dinner and relax. On one occasion, Lionel brought a roast for our friends to grill. He was full of energy and fun. A couple of years after moving to Atlanta, I received a call from the same friend inviting my then wife and me to be a guest at Lionel's table for the Coca-Cola 75th Annual Celebration where he would be playing. It was amazing, here is a man in his eighties, shuffling along, appearing decrepit, but when Lionel practiced on the drums, he became alive. His hand speed and dexterity on the drums were amazing. During the actual event Lionel's energy as he played the drums and vibraphone was captivating. He was still the showman doing his thing, an older man doing something he loved and doing it well. A lesson to remember. There were celebrities at the event. Merv Griffin, entertainer and creator of *Wheel of Fortune* and *Jeopardy* shows, and movie star Zsa Zsa Gabor were at the table in front of where we were sitting. They were having big fun, just as carefree as you would want to be. It appeared to me that White people with fame and fortune enjoy themselves at a much different level than us common folks. Also, I saw for the first time what true White Privilege and wealth looked like. After the impressive celebration, we returned to the hotel where Lionel was staying. Although he was tired, sitting on his bed he began to reminisce about his life. Lionel talked about his concerns as to who would write his autobiography. Again, like Leo Durocher, Lionel shared stories about past men and women jazz artists such as Benny Goodman, Sarah Vaughan, Dianah Washington, and Lena Horne, with whom he played and/or discovered. Lionel was a man of music, not a businessman per se. His late wife handled their business affairs. However, later on I became aware that he was politically well connected. Just talking about his concerns and life was a humbling experience. Why was I in that position at that time dining and listening to an American jazz icon talking to me about a few of his life experiences and concerns? Later I could only conclude that I was where I was supposed to be. Keep going.

It was exciting for me to play tennis, attended Afrocentric lectures, Black-produced theater plays, parties, art exhibits sponsored by African American businesses and universities. I enjoyed meeting African American entertainers and politicians from all over the country who came to Atlanta to participate in the Black experience.

It was in Atlanta where I also enjoyed and learned that women were equally competitive in business, politics, and sports. In Indianapolis I considered myself to be a decent tennis player. I met a couple of women who said they could play. One such person, an attractive flight attendant, beat me every time we played. At first my pride was deeply offended that a woman beat me, but after playing tennis with a couple other women, it occurred to me that tennis took not only muscles, but also practice and skill, and these female tennis players deserved the same respect as men tennis players. I also figured out that I had to adjust my attitude about who was the stronger sex. In Atlanta I came in contact with a wider range of African American men and women who were competing at all levels. It became obvious that in the South, respectful behavior was highly valued, along with a sense of humility and competency.

As my social life picked up, I enjoyed Atlanta's exciting social life. All the African American men and women I met socially from all parts of the country and from different backgrounds cannot be adequately covered, although a few instances stand out in my memory. One day at lunch with a colleague in downtown Atlanta, I saw a woman at another table finishing lunch. She was poised, conservatively dressed, and had an impressive shape; the kind of woman one would see in a TV commercial. I excused myself and went over to where she was sitting and introduced myself with as much confidence that I could generate. With a beautiful smile and charm, she told me that she was going back to work. Not knowing if I would ever see her again, I asked if we could meet the next day after work for drinks, and she agreed. Wow! I was impressed with my shy self and left the restaurant with my chest stuck out.

The following day, she and I met and enjoyed a nice conversation. She had moved to Atlanta from Alabama and was finding her way in the new city. I indicated that I recently moved from Indiana. Shortly after that we began to see each other frequently, enjoying each other's company. One evening she hesitantly asked me for a favor. It was obvious that she seemed worried. It turned out that she needed money as soon as possible. I was surprised at such a request, as it seemed that things were going well for both of us. My inner voice seemed to take control. A red warning flag went up, because something didn't seem right. I suggested that we get together in a couple of days and that we would talk about the matter which she agreed. When we met a couple of days later, I noticed that she looked tired, her energy and smile were absent. Although I was deeply concerned about her well- being, I told her that I would not lend her the money. In a most fatalistic manner, she said that she understood. A few days passed, and when I called a couple of times, I got no answer. Through a mutual friend I later learned that she had become hooked on cocaine, was not doing well, and had moved, address unknown. I was surprised, hurt, and wonder how I could have missed warning signs that she was using drugs. There was nothing that I could do but keep going and hope for the best for her, but it was sad to learn of her situation. My inner voice was present when I needed it, as the whole situation could have led me down a different path. I pray that she survived her demons.

# STRIP CLUB EXPERIENCE

There was another time that stands out in my mind when life had more in store to test if I was learning anything. With a couple of friends I went to one of the hottest Black strip clubs in Atlanta. Before people were allowed to enter, a security guard checked to see if anyone was carrying a weapon. Then you were allowed to go to the window inside to pay to enter the main entrance where there was another big mean-looking security guard. Inside the club there were the curious. There were professionals looking to relieve stress. There were some who appeared to be outside the law, flashing rolls of money. There were the blue- and white-collar guys wanting to be part of the excitement of seeing well-built young women almost entirely naked and doing their thing. Some of the strippers/dancers were working to pay for their college education and support their families. More than a few of them were from rural areas of Georgia, Florida, Alabama, and the Carolinas trying for a new start in hot Atlanta. From a male's point of view, it was a beautiful and stimulating sight to see!

One of the strippers apparently took an interest in me. She came by and spoke to us briefly, went away and then came back, it was part of their job when not on stage. She pulled up a chair behind me to have a conversation, which was different. Although I thought it was out of the ordinary for someone in her position to take the time just to talk without performing for money I didn't take it seriously until one of my partners gave me a look as if to ask What is going on?

My other friend said, "Ah, shit."

After she excused herself, both my partners mentioned that she appeared to be genuinely interested in me, a thought I nervously dismissed. Part of her job was to move around unless asked to perform at that table. What was unusual is she sat directly behind me and communicated in a manner not common for strippers. Strippers make their money by being in front of men, not behind them. A short time later she returned, introducing herself. Again, sitting behind me and leaning forward, she struck up a general conversation that was like two people meeting in a park. She excused herself again, saying that she would return later, and she did. At that time she asked if I was interested in getting together for lunch. What was going on? She seemed sincere enough. As it turned out she had another job and was working at the club to make additional money. I asked myself was this some kind of setup. If anything went wrong, my job at the medical school could be in jeopardy. I agreed to lunch. My partners were as curious as I was. The woman in her mid-twenties was articulate and did not fit the so-call stripper stereotype, whatever that was. She and I met for lunch and had a good conversation. When it was time to leave, we agreed to have lunch again. At that point, I was confused as to what should I do if the relation took on its own energy. Here I was having lunch and obviously impressed with a nice-looking, mature, and intelligent woman who worked in a strip club. Although I was somewhat conservative Catholic when it came to money matters, decorum, and wild socializing, my male instincts were pushing me toward her. Why not? It wasn't about love; it was experiencing an adventure with a woman who know more about life than myself. What in the hell was I doing? It finally came to me that I needed to maintain control some kind of control, no matter what. We met again, and this time it was clear to me that she was interested in pursuing a meaningful relationship. For the third time in my life, I had to find the courage to walk away. I told her that we could not continue to meet because things could turn serious, and neither one of us was ready to deal with that situation. Damn! I was impressed with her serious calmness, as my instincts did not pick up insincerity on her part. Matter of fact, I was scared and felt guilty for what was coming out of my mouth. I was looking for her to express anger or show a bad attitude, but she was together. Sometimes I look back and wonder about her. Something about her was special. I like to think that the human being I met in a strip club is doing well. I guess that we were passing pilgrims on our respective life journeys.

It became obvious to me that it was time to settle down, as too much of a good thing was not physically, socially, or mentally healthy.

# GOING INTO MARRIAGE AGAIN

I eventually met and started dating on a serious basis an outgoing woman from Atlanta who was a flight attendant. She was attractive, charming, and religious; a true Georgia Peach born and raised in Atlanta. During the time we dated, I met her family. Her father, a very religious and congenial man, was a self-taught carpenter and knew how to build a house from the ground up. With a heart of a lion, he raised one boy and two girls after his wife left the family. My wife in her early twenties had attended college for a brief period, but dropped out when she had an opportunity to be among the first African American women to be hired by a major airline as a flight attendant. She flew all over the country and was able to support herself in the manner she wanted. She was the pride of her family.

Although we were from different social and education backgrounds, we liked to have fun as well as enjoy life up to a point, and I was ready to settle down. However, I must admit that I heard a whisper asking if I was sure about marrying that particular person. Regardless of my uneasiness, we married. Prior to our marriage, I was startled when my fiancée wanted our wedding announcement in *Jet Magazine*. That did not happen, but we had a nice formal wedding with my former roommate serving as best man. The wedding was well attended by our current friends, including several from Indianapolis, my bride's family, my mother, and some of the Morehouse School of Medicine family.

We began to build a new life together, first living in a nice apartment in Smyrna, Georgia, where there were tulips of all colors, other beautiful flowers, tall Georgia pines, and bamboo trees. There was a good-sized lake with ducks and geese floating majestically along. Sitting by the lake was a place where one could enjoy nature and relax. After a couple of years of apartment living, we took our next step and built a house. We attended a religiously nourishing Methodist Church with a lot of energy and an inspirational pastor. I soon began to attend Bible Study class. The leader of the class, who became a friend (another angel), must have recognized that I was on a soul-searching journey. He worked at IBM, a gentle person who was very knowledgeable of the Bible and shared his spiritual insights. He was a constant source of encouragement and inspiration, as my wife and I were personally struggling. Our understanding of life was different. She had never been married, had no children to love and nurture, and coming up very poor, she understood how to take care of herself at a level she never had experienced. Being asked to become a team player through the sanctity of marriage was asking too much from her. As a backdrop, my dad in Indianapolis was suffering from a stroke, one daughter was in college, and I was paying support for my other daughter. I was making money, but it was going out in every direction. My wife and I had built a very nice house in Decatur, Georgia, and I paid most of the household bills. The organizational and social demands of the medical school were intense. I was the oldest on both sides of the family and took my responsibilities seriously toward responding to them. I would travel frequently back and forth to Indianapolis and for the medical school.

From the beginning we attended church. I began to listen and study the Bible, which awakened within me better understanding of the meaning of love, hope, faith, and charity. However, I was still a long way from spiritual understanding and religious culture, because there was too much on my physical life plate. Too much! But Ruben, my friend and Bible study teacher provided a place for contemplation, peace, and a better understanding of teachings from the Bible. To this day I appreciate him for taking the time to help me on my way.

After we built the house, we agreed that it was not a good fit for us and negotiated return of that house back to the builder, who sold it in no time. It turned out that we made the right decision, as the development was over built. We then found another new residential division that had everything that we wanted. The development was hilly and had tall Georgia pines. What made it even more ideal was there were African Americans from across the country who would be our neighbors. Wow! There were deer, foxes, and rabbits roaming about in the nearby woods. At night one could smell fresh air and see the stars and Stone Mountain, where the Ku Klux Klan had held their rallies a decade earlier. My instincts and overall feeling of wellbeing indicated that we were in the right place.

I worked with the contractor on the layout of the house, a job I found to be fun. We believed that we were where we belonged. It was a dream come true, as neither one of us had lived in a new house with all the modern trimmings. I became involved in establishing the development's homeowner's association, which was a challenge in every sense of the word. The HOA had to assume from the developer responsibility for HOA-required funds previously collected and set rules and regulations as to how the subdivision functioned, that included assessments of fees and fines, collection of dues, and overseeing the nonresidential part of the property swimming pool, clubhouse, and tennis courts. The coming together of people of color from different parts of the country with diverse and varied educational backgrounds made putting the HOA together a pleasure and a very demanding challenge. Many people had their own ideas as to what they wanted. Finding compromise while following HOA-proposed guidelines gave me the opportunity to gain additional experience and to make some close friends, many of whom wanted to do the right thing.

My wife continued to fly full-time, and I was putting in fifty-plus hours per week at the medical school. Periodically I was traveling on school business as well as driving 500 miles to Indianapolis to pick up my daughters, something I always looked forward to with great joy. All this was no problem, as I was accustomed to wearing several hats at once. I loved it all.

One of our neighbors was a marketing representative for Darrell Strawberry of the Los Angeles Dodgers and two other Dodgers. At a party I had the opportunity to converse with Darrell. I found him to be introspective and surprisingly reserved. When the Dodgers were in town to play the Atlanta Braves, a couple of them would come out to my neighbor's house to relax and later go to planned parties, including a very popular strip club. Believe me, there is nothing like being around professional athletes, especially at parties and restaurants. They have to deal with a lot of pressures and temptations. Too much of a good thing can mess you up.

In preparation for a Halloween Party, my wife and I went to a downtown Marietta costume shop. There the KKK was marching around the city square, for what reason I did not know. It was the first time that I had ever seen the Klan up close and personally. While state law allowed them to dress in the Klan uniform, they were not allowed to be masked. While we were in the costume shop, a little boy and his mother came into the store, both in their Klan uniforms. Their outfits were the whitest clothing that I had ever seen. My wife obviously was nervous and told me not to look at them, but I couldn't help staring at them. Strange as it may seem, I felt pity for both of them. They appeared to be of poor bearing, with blank eyes showing little expression, as if the people were merely going through the motion of living. There was no sense of purpose or anger. They came in, looked around, and left to rejoin their group.

After several years of a roller-coaster marriage, it came to an end. We were two very different individuals who had not adequately understood what it took to make a marriage work. In looking back at our marriage, I was repeating what my father and mother experienced, going through separation and divorce. My wife had come from an economically depressed background, and her obvious intentions were to enjoy the material things in life as best she could and survive. My vision deep within was to strive and build on the previous day's challenges and climb the next mountain.

While we were married we enjoyed getting together with our friends, traveling, and having family gatherings. A couple of our friends were cast members in the TV series *In the Heat of the Night* and were involved in the Black actor's theater. Our exposure to African Americans, most of whom were striving to develop their skills and talents, was awesome. In Atlanta I was able to observe that there was a unique bond of togetherness southern style, where the families and immediate friends played, prayed, ate, and enjoyed life on an everyday basis.

After ten years my employment at the medical school was coming to an end, as the objectives for which I was employed had been achieved. I was saddened in leaving that warm and yet challenging environment where I found another part of my undiscovered self. I would miss most the friendly people who had also helped me to grow my confidence and over all maturity. All of the above life happenings involved such a variety of life experiences. In Atlanta I was in the right place at the right time in my life. Per the Universal clock, it was time to continue my journey of self-discovery. There was more to come.

# COMING BACK HOME

Meanwhile, in Indianapolis, my mother's physical and mental condition had become a major concern. It seemed to me that my personal, marital, and occupational challenges were teaming up on me all at the same time. What was going on? I heard no internal voices to guide or encourage me. Now, more than thirty years later, I have no doubt that the reasons why I heard no inner voices was that anger, confusion, fear, and self-doubt were in control. The faith, hope, and love that I thought I had seemed to be periodically absent and in need of improvement. For the first time in my life, I did not hear an inner voice. My inner confidence was taking a holiday, thanks to me allowing it to go. It was an ass kicking that took me years to recover from. Was it my out-of-whack ego blocking my positive inner visions?

Although I wanted to remain in Atlanta after my employment with the school ended, it became obvious that my marriage had come to an unfortunate end, and I had no choice but to return to my home state and tend to the immediate personal and medical needs of my mother. I did not want to leave Atlanta; however, by being back home, the silver lining was that I would be closer to my lovely daughters. One had graduated from college, and the other had completed her undergraduate degree and was moving on to her master's degree. Likewise, I would later meet my future wife, whom I had met more than twenty years earlier. I also looked forward to renewing old friendships. I was somewhat aware that I had changed, and I did not know how I would be received. I did not understand that at that time, change was part of the essence of life and that my friends had also changed. I just had to keep going regardless of any circumstances or obstacles.

How I was going to earn a living was a major concern. It seemed that the prevailing thinking was to pick up where I left off. Very few of my friends or associates asked me about my ten-year experience in Atlanta, nor did most of them seem to care who I was or what I had learned there. There was very little conversation about life, little acknowledgment of our inner selves; just going about at life as usual. I expected more, which was my problem, not theirs; however, I got the feeling that the challenge was to prove to them and myself that I belonged in my hometown, but belonged to what I had no idea. What in God's name was going on?

As confusion and concern began to again take hold, I was confronted with my own three S's: Strange and Shitty, and the Simplicity. My intuition warned me that, damn, nearly everything and everyone had changed, and that included me. What is going on? A life lesson was that as the world turns there are changes, always. I was beginning to learn the importance of faith, hope, and charity. In the past they were only words that I read in the Bible and heard at church. I found myself again on my knees praying. Thank God for my daughters! They helped me gain more sense of love, especially when it came to dealing with my mother's unpredictable behavior. I was slowly getting clues as to what was going on in my life, but the fog and noise in my mind were ever present. My nights were restless; there were noises going on in my head and sleep was limited.

My mother, who did not raise me, was in obvious mental and physical decline. Mom and I for the first time since I was three years old were now living under the same roof; how strange. Although I did not realize it at the time, our roles had changed. I was becoming the parent and mom the child. I would not recommend that kind of transition to anyone. Neither one of us liked the position in which life had placed us. My mother was slow to take directions from anyone, let alone her son. In many cases I was the object of her frustration and anger. Very painful, especially coming from a mother. Nowhere to run and nowhere to hide!

# GOING INTO BUSINESS (1990S)

As TIME marched on, and in accordance with the Universal plan, help came from a White person I did not know, but we did have mutual friends. He offered me a business opportunity in insurance that was an answer to my prayers. The entire opportunity came out of the blue. Most importantly, that person introduced me to his family, close friends, and associates. Most of them gave freely of their time and shared valuable information, while at the same time wondering why the patriarch of the family was giving me such an opportunity. The answer was for one, the person who asked me to join him had already made his money in the insurance business and loved the challenge of helping someone else to do the same. He introduced me to contacts and gave me the opportunity to learn and interact in a market reserved for primarily White male operatives. Two, he was a nonconformist and an adventurer with a big heart that was not always apparent. He possessed good instinctive skills, was very creative, and understood people and insurance products. He became a mentor and later a friend. I was provided an office with file cabinets, phone, desktop computer, and supplies. While having little to no exposure in life, health, extraordinary risk, property, and, liability insurance, I studied and passed the state licensing test for health, life, property and casualty insurance. I made every effort to learn new terminology, insurance contracts, and legal ramifications regarding liability and

## GOING INTO BUSINESS (1990S)

negligence. I was trying to learn every possible area of the insurance and marketing business regardless of the specialty. The insurance products also included extraordinary risk insurance, which involved European insurance companies as well as American specialty insurance carriers, large and small. Actually I had bitten off more than I could chew, but fortunately I didn't know the difference.

In the area of sales, I learned to identify a person or organization with a particular insurance need, identify the insurance carrier that specialized in that particular market, negotiate the premium, if possible, make the presentation, and close the deal. I was given the opportunity to have confidence in my thinking process in an entirely new professional field. If something went wrong, I found out what the problem was, made the correction, and moved on, since rejection was part of the game. I discovered as an African American man I could participate on a larger stage and that White men made mistakes like everybody else. It was confirmed in my own mind that I was in no way inferior to White men. Somewhat of a revelation! However, my fears and anxieties were a constant companion. Where there is fear there is doubt. Having to prove oneself over and over again can make or break a person mentally as well as physically.

Although I was given an opportunity to become self-employed, I was in need of startup capital. With little extra money of my own to live on, I contacted a White friend I had formerly worked with at the medical school and who I intuitively trusted through the years. Without any hesitation, he loaned me several hundred dollars, a loan I repaid within three years, as promised. With my $500, a cash advance on my charge card, and my friend's loan, I formally started business. That friend, his wife, and his daughters are my friends to this day.

Back home again, I had to adjust socially and learn as much as possible in order to be self-sustaining. At the same time, I had to take on my greatest personal task, how to be patient in taking care of my birth mother who was losing her battle with dementia. How could I express my deep anger and feelings of abandonment to a person who could no longer acknowledge her own feelings? What frustrations! Where was the love? I had to just suck it up and continue doing what I had always been doing: staggering forward. The desire to be loved is a constant challenge.

During my working and after hours, the entire experience of trying to be positive while enduring a high degree of stress cannot be adequately expressed within this narrative. I was developing a competitive business and addressing the needs of my mother I never really knew, while witnessing Alzheimer taking its toll with her. What a painful disease to witness with its helplessness, mental anguish, and the heart aches. To caregivers of the world, you have my prayers.

To start an insurance business and renew old friendships as well as make new acquaintances was a new beginning. But then I had the opportunities of being with my two grown daughters, two grandsons, two aunts, cousins, and my sister and brother from Dad's second marriage. I appreciated them more than ever. My daughters were grown and were making their own way in life. My inner voice encouraged me to get to know them again as individuals the best I could as I continued to experience a sense of guilt for not being with them when they may have needed me the most. In short I felt that it was Annie, in her own voice, encouraging me onward and not to lose faith. I am sure that I confused some people as to where I was coming from, but that was part of my journey. For it can be confusing to search for your purpose in life, trying to understand why things are the way they are while trying to meet your needs as a human being and find some happiness.

What came out of my caregiver experience with my mother was a beginning lesson in patience, humility, and prayer. I was also beginning to learn how to face my own fears. While back in my hometown, I began to attend several churches in search of spiritual connection, which something inside me was encouraging me to do. After visiting several churches and enjoying some of the preaching and gospel singing, one day I bumped into a friend on a downtown street, someone I had not seen in many years. Ken had recently started a Bible study he held in his home. He invited me to attend and without hesitation I said I would be there. I began to attend Bible study on a regular basis. I did not know at the time that this meeting on a downtown street would be a giant step toward my search for God. Ken was very dedicated to the teachings from the Bible, and the small group that came together once a week provided a sense of love and faith. One of the attendees was an elderly woman who became for me a symbol of love and peace. I called her mom. She was someone I desperately needed in my life, especially at that time. She calmed my agitated spirit. I listened and observed her unshakable demeanor and faith. We remained close until her death years later. She was an angel in every sense of the word, a reminder of Annie. My inner voice assured me that I was in the right place and with people who had love for mankind and faith in God. God is Love and Love is God. It was something more than religious; it was spiritual. I was being moved past the Catholic ritual, practices, and procedures into another stage of religious spirituality. I was beginning to understand that there was a spiritual part in me of which I was only somewhat aware. I needed to study more, pray, and learn from those who were further along the road in search of God.

At that point in my life the practice of yoga was still a few years away. What I learned in California regarding Higher Consciousness had not yet sunk into my overall consciousness.

# THE INSURANCE BUSINESS

Besides learning the insurance business, which was a lot of work, I was one of the few African Americans being taught in specialty areas. Some Whites seemed skeptical as to my ability to acquire the technical aspects of the insurance business.

My preparation to meet such challenges had already been laid out for me, through my primary and secondary Catholic education, undergraduate and graduate studies, and my professional and community experiences: banking, the chamber of commerce, department director in state government, international travels, civil rights activities, nonprofit organizations, as well as a member of several boards, and as an administrator for two medical schools. I only then began to realize how far I had come thanks to my guardian angels, a few friends, and many prayers that Mother Father God of the Universe give light to the path I was on. I never forgot that I stood on the shoulders of others, and without them I would not be able to climb toward my destiny.

During the fourth year, my insurance business and my confidence began to pick up. During that time I was in partnership with my mentor and friend. Through him I was able to work with some of the larger national and international insurance groups. Although I sold health, life, and auto insurance, my main focus as well as that of my partner was the extraordinary risk insurance.

## THE INSURANCE BUSINESS

This kind of insurance demanded more creativity and resourcefulness. This small powerful specialized market is highly competitive. I loved the various challenges, and it was a serious adventure. Why I loved it I am not sure; the journey was stressful while at the same time rewarding. To stay in the game, international calls to European insurers were necessary, and travels to New York; Philadelphia; Jackson, Mississippi; Detroit; Chicago; Denver; and Washington, D.C. were always an adventure. I could have done a better job with my various insurance endeavors, but family, social, and community activities at times interfered with my ability to focus and be the best that I could be in a specialized area of insurance. However, I have no complaints as to my overall intentions and business endeavors. During this period, I found that with more confidence, I could accomplish what I thought was beyond my abilities. However, there was no denying that in sales living with the reality of rejection is an everyday event. As an inner-city African American man, it was very difficult for me and at times felt very personal when I heard that potential clients were not interested in my competitive proposal or that they had selected a competitor or declined to do business with me. It was like salt being poured into an open wound. Were the rejections of my proposals because I was African American? Did my proposal fall short, or what? I chose to develop a thick skin, which was required at all times.

My partner asked if I would consider being recommended for membership to join the prestigious Columbia Club, a private predominately White club of local political—mostly Republican—and business movers and shakers. In fact they were the system. This club brought back negative memories of when as a boy and lived one mile from the downtown establishment where Negroes could work only as waiters or janitors. The front entrance was guarded by a doorman in a red uniform. Annie and Uncle George's next-door neighbor in the flat, Mr. Bill, worked at the club as a waiter. A slender, articulate, neat man, he was very good at providing service as a waiter to influential White business men. As a child I admired his dignity and how he carried himself.

The thought of being a member of the Columbia Club caused me to fear White intimidation and/or rejection as an African American. Who wants to be stared at in an unwelcome manner or treated as a second-class member?

Regardless of my high anxiety, I had to step up and go forward. My advice is to walk tall and look people in the room straight in the eye. I would find a way to own my space and not be intimidated. Like it or not, it was a business opportunity. I decided to join the club. Internally I was encouraged to join, as it would honor Mr. Bill, the waiter, the man and my hero, a Black giant. God bless him.

My mother's mental as well as physical condition continued to rapidly decline. We both struggled with the realization that we were in a downward spiral. One day Mom was nice and the next day she was accusing me of stealing her money and that she was calling the police. At times she would knock on my bedroom door very angry. In her state of mind, Mom found curse words that I did not know existed. I either prepared her meals or brought food home for her to eat until she lost her sense of taste and did not know what kind of food she wanted. Very sad. I helped her put on her clothes and cleaned up urine whenever and wherever it was. Even though my daughters had their own families, they were a tremendous help, thank God. On occasion a few neighbors helped as best they could. One day when I was returning from the office, I saw fire trucks and police cars in front of the house. My heart was in my throat as I tried to remain calm. Mom had tried to cook something and left the skillet burning and filled the house with smoke. As the firemen were leaving the house, the captain gave me a stern look and warned that she should not be left alone. That look made me feel guilty. I had already become very concerned that I could not leave her alone. Efforts to have someone come in on a part-time basis had not worked out. It became clear that I could no longer take care of Mom at home, even though I wanted to take care of her. Letting go? The thought of actually placing her in a caretaker facility was heart wrenching, but I felt I had no choice. She did not want to be there, and the anguished look on her face could have pierced the hearts of many. Words cannot express the pain we both felt. Because of that painful experience, though, I am able to minister with compassion and empathy to those going through similar situations. I can listen to other caregivers, understand their personal challenges and pain; and let them know that they are not alone, which gives me the opportunity to help other human beings as I was helped. I wondered who takes care of the caregiver?

# THE INSURANCE BUSINESS

My attempts at dating obviously did not go as well as I would have liked. There was too much going on in my life, although there were a few women that I wish that I could have met under better circumstances. Yet I had friends who made an impact on my life and who believed in me, for which I am very grateful. These precious few friends provided comfort and a place in their homes where I could briefly relax and just be myself. An established women's social group invited a couple of close friends and me to attend a dinner dance held in Hilton Head, South Carolina. It was one of the few times since returning to Indianapolis that I had an opportunity to get away, socialize, relax, and meet other people. During the three-day weekend, I met through other friends nationally known journalist Bernard Shaw, the first Black news anchor with CNN. Several of us guys, including Bernie, got together in one of the host hotel suites to watch a sports event on television. As we relaxed, had drinks, and watched television, Bernie and I talked in general about various things, but I noticed he had a controlled smiled. It did not occur to me at the time that Bernard Shaw, a man with a serious demeanor, carried a load on his shoulders on another level that the rest of us could not imagine. It was great to be in the company of confident African American males who were just trying to enjoy the moment before going back to New York; D.C.; Cincinnati; Columbia, South Carolina; Atlanta and other places to face their reality of being professional Black men in America. What an experience to feel the energy level and joy of being among common Blacks folks moving up the American ladder and temporarily free!

# LONDON, PARIS, ZURICH, VENICE EXPERIENCE

A female friend I was dating at that time asked if I would be interested in traveling to Europe with her son and his friend. The thinking was that I could help manage the boys and give us the opportunity to experience Europe together. It was our destiny to take the trip, and to this day I appreciate our adventure and the boys. In London we visited the British Museum, Hyde Park, Piccadilly Square, and Chinatown. Traveling by train to Paris, France, through the Chunnel underneath the English Channel was a shared excitement for all of us. Paris: how can one describe that beautiful and romantic city, to have wine at outdoor cafés and to be part of the city environment was joyous. We visited the Louvre Museum, seeing in awe the *Mona Lisa* painting. Viewing Paris from atop the Eiffel Tower is a once-in-a-lifetime experience. Attending mass at Notre Dame de Paris cathedral was a religious and spiritual event for me. I felt that I was caught-up in time and space. On to Zurich we went by Eurail, another unique experience. Zurich, Switzerland, is an international financial center and cosmopolitan city. As an African American in the insurance business, I needed to get a feel for one of the major satellites of capitalism. Traveling by train from Zurich, seeing the snow-caped Alps, and going to Venice and Florence, Italy, fulfilled my deep yearning to see that part of the world. The world is a beautiful place.

# A MOTHER'S PASSING

Six years after I returned to Indianapolis from Atlanta to take care of my mother and having already gone through a second divorce, my mother died. I had been a caregiver long enough to feel not only a sense of loss, but also guilt for not being able to do enough. Mom and I never got to say that we loved each other or give each other a hug. The several weeks after her passing, I had trouble falling to sleep and would wake up at night and go to the empty bedroom to check on her. It was very difficult to immediately shut off my anxieties, and perhaps more importantly, a sense of loss. It took time. Eventually I came to the conclusion that Mom was no longer in need of me. Later I would fall into a deep sleep not realizing the extent of my exhaustion and depression.

As life would have it, I had come up from Atlanta in 1988 and was at Dad's bedside when he took his last breath. Twelve years later I arrived at the same hospital a half hour after Mom took her last breath. It was strange after not living with either of them since the age of three. The only proximity for the three of us was the same hospital only a floor apart when they died. Spending time in the hospital room with them after death was profound. So many thoughts flooded my mind, including thoughts of sadness, anger, love, and remorse, which I could not explain. Those thoughts scared me.

What happens when pain, suffering, depression, and sorrow all collide at the same time? How does one maintain a sense of self and resolve to walk boldly without falling further into the abyss of despair? These are questions that have been asked by mankind many times before. However, when mental, physical, and spiritual challenges knock at your own door, it is very personal when there is a sense of your own survival involved. When I slept, I had troubling noises going on in my head, none of which made any sense. I can only explain the noises like being in an automobile body shop with all of the hammering and banging, which left me troubled, tired, and fearful in the morning. These noises began soon after I returned to Indianapolis and continued for years. Mild to severe gout attacks increased in frequency, especially at night. At times I walked to the office despite my pain, and I dragged my affected leg like a mummy in horror films. I was in too much pain to be embarrassed. It wasn't pretty. I knew only one thing: that I had to keep going forward. What other choice did I have? I am sure my roller coaster behavior was confusing to some immediate family members, close friends, and female friends, as my anxieties were on display. But I am also thankful that there were people who came into my life who were caring as well as supportive. Universal God provides shelter from life's adversity by providing help. For me, I was in search of God, but did not actually understand how or where to search. The spiritual psychic Edgar Cayce explains life as in the physical, mental, and spiritual. Is it ultimately about realigning our bodies with the mental and connecting with our souls, which is the goal of our journey to come full circle from whence we came?

I found myself on my knees trying to pray and communicate with God, but I did not know how to communicate with God. I still did not understand meditation well. I prayed outwardly, not realizing that there was already love and protection coming from within. The spiritual communication involving my soul and mind was already present through a power that I had yet to understand. Working through one's sorrow and pain takes time, but the time that it took to go forward was a blessing, as I was just beginning to understand and have some faith in God's grace and mercy.

Based on my journey so far, I have come to a few conclusions. We humans are challenged every day to withstand the physical bombardment of anger, sex, and greed. Our God-given egos have a meaningful purpose, but we must find a way to balance this gift with love, forgiveness, and a positive use of our freewill. There were good days and then not-so-good days when one too many bricks were thrown my way. Now there is a difference. As a unique representative of the Universe, which we all are, I was in the process of becoming aware of the importance of faith, love, and understanding of my life's purpose. There was more joy and confidence in confronting the many challenges and my mistakes.

Shortly after the death of my mother, I experienced pain in my knee that grew worse over time that resulted in going to a doctor. The diagnosis was a torn meniscus that required surgery. Although the knee surgery was successful, my hamstring muscles completely locked up, which required additional physical therapy and extended my time on crutches. When I was alone in the house with limited mobility, my emotional challenges increased. Not able to go to the office, I had limited client contact. Driving to the doctor's office and going for physical therapy while on crutches also contributed to my feelings of helplessness and at times despair, as my physical abilities were noticeably diminished. Blessings and angels, including my daughters came at various times to let me know that I was not alone. Others also came by to check on me, brought food, and ran errands for me. Some who came by were a complete surprise. I saw support coming from people who I wasn't aware that they cared. These expressions of love, it helps.

# ANOTHER CLOSE CALL; BICYCLE FREEFALL

As I began to become more confident in my new occupation as an insurance broker, I took up jogging and biking. A group of insurance colleagues, including my insurance partner, decided to ride our bikes south of Columbus, Indiana, through the countryside. It was a challenge for me, as I had not ridden a bike for any distance in several years; therefore, I needed to get a bike tune-up. When I went to pick up my bike at the bicycle shop, the owner asked if I had a helmet. My initial response was that I did not need a helmet. The woman seemed concerned and directed me to the helmets. I was a little annoyed that she was so insistent to make a sale. When I was about to repeat that I did not want the helmet, my inner voice told me to buy the helmet. The voice was so absolute that I immediately picked the helmet up and purchased it without looking at the price. As I walked out of the shop with my bike and helmet, I felt relieved. I was happy to have my tuned-up bike and my first ever helmet.

It was a nice sunny day when our group biked through Indiana farmlands that included wading in a shallow river. The country roads and corn fields made for beautiful scenery. I had never seen such tall corn stalks. I was so impressed that I decided to take a picture with my camera that was wrapped around the front of my handlebar. As I reached for the camera, my front wheel turned sideways. The bike stopped and projected me head first over the handlebar. As

I was flying up and over the handlebar, I knew that I was in a bad spot and the woman's advice at the bike shop flashed before me. Then it was lights out. I was unconscious for a period of time. I was on the ground hearing people around me, some in somewhat of a panic, and then I heard the ambulance siren, and passed out. At the hospital, I was lying on a gurney in the emergency room and people were talking. To this day I don't remember if an X-ray was taken. The doctor told me that I had a concussion and could stay overnight for observation or return to Indianapolis to see my doctor. He told me that I was fortunate to have had on a helmet and gave me pain medication that put me in a foggy state for two days. The woman friend I was dating and my Jewish colleague and friend were my angels who gave me tender loving care. I am not sure if I went to my doctor once I returned to Indianapolis. I should have gone to my doctor for a follow up, but why I didn't go is a mystery. Perhaps, the superman syndrome influenced my thinking. Again, through the grace of Universal God I was saved from a potentially fatal accident and related long-term brain damage. Two weeks after recuperating from my injuries, I returned to the bike shop along with Ken, my Bible instructor. I told that same human being who demanded that I get the helmet what had happened and thanked her for being my angel. To this day, I remember her face and what she said and how she said it, and I am very grateful.

I soon discovered that my bicycle ordeal was not yet over. As a result of landing on my head—the helmet and right shoulder absorbed the most impact. My shoulder required surgery. I began to experience pain in my shoulder to such a point that I saw a surgeon friend, who immediately diagnosed that I had suffered a fractured clavicle and needed surgery for repair and placement of a screw. Again I went under the knife and later went back to physical therapy. Still recuperating from surgery for a torn meniscus, I had to wear an arm sling, all while I tried to work from home and take care of my deceased mother's financial and personal matters. I had to learn how to use my left hand. Plus, I continued to walk with a limp. What a strange kind of physical experience.

After my mother's death, a bicycle accident, and two surgeries, I felt that I could enter into a serious relationship. What a roller coaster ride! The old socially self-confident person had undergone some life changes. There were gaps in my existence as a living entity. Something was missing, and I didn't know what it was. Had my mental fog and fear returned with a vengeance to confuse me?

I met and dated a couple of very nice women who were fun to be with, and who helped me gain some life perspective piece by piece. However, I was not ready to settle down, as my mind and spirit were restless. I was not at peace. Was I having a problem loving myself? I had miles to go.

# INDIANA SAND DUNES

Another adventure that almost had a fatal ending happened when I accompanied a friend to Chicago with a stopover in LaPorte, Indiana. The sight of Lake Michigan was overwhelming. Excited, I decided to jog ahead to enjoy the beauty of the lake and sand dunes. I decided to run up one of the taller sand dunes, because it seemed challenging, and it was something that I had never done. Halfway up I found the shifting sands more challenging than I thought, but my ego pushed me forward. Once at the top of the dune, I caught only a brief view of the beautiful surroundings before the sand gave way under me and suddenly I was sinking fast. I had never heard of quicksand atop of a sand dune. I immediately realized that I was in serious trouble, and with one lunge, I was able to get a foot on firmer sand, pull the other leg up, and roll until I was able to stand without sinking. I had to descend on the backside of the dunes where the footing was firmer. My friend could tell I was stressed and asked what was wrong. A year later I read in the newspaper that a boy had climbed one of the taller sand dunes and disappeared beneath the quick sand. It took rescue workers some time to find a way to stabilize the dune and rescue the boy, who tragically was found dead. Again, I was reminded how close I came to suffering the same fate. I wondered and asked myself why God had let the boy die and not me. Then I remembered *The Purpose Driven Life*: The purpose of life lies neither in the questions, nor in the answers. We can ask the questions in hopes that the answers will bring us comfort, relief, a sense of knowing or help us move forward. But for me, as the book suggests, living life purposely renders the questions and answers as no longer relevant.

# PHILADELPHIA STORY

My insurance mentor and partner arranged for a meeting in Philadelphia with a successful African American insurance broker I had worked with in my capacity as director of human resources at the medical school in Atlanta. My partner also set up a business meeting with an old colleague he had known many years earlier. The colleague was an old school salesman who had been associated with Ray Kroc, who purchased the McDonald's Corporation. The story that I heard was Kroc offered a region of McDonald's to his fellow salesman once the franchises were established. My partner's colleague accepted the deal and went on to become a multimillionaire. My partner arranged for us to stay at the Four Seasons Hotel in downtown Philly. It was the first time that I had stayed in such a swank hotel, especially for an inner-city kid. We met my partner's friend for breakfast in the hotel dining area. He was a big rough and tough White guy from Polish background. He spoke in a loud voice laced with curse words for emphasis. Intimidating, to say the least. As I watched and listened in awe at their conversation, I immediately recognized that I was being taken to school by two old-school wealthy White Mad Men entrepreneurs. The rough and tough millionaire guy asked my partner how many airplanes he had owned. To my surprise my partner said that he had owned a few. The big guy said he was down to one plane after owning three.

After their reminiscing, the waitress asked if we were ready to order. She appeared to be nervous. The big guy asked if there was anything wrong. With hesitation and looking back at her manager, she said that he had been getting on her. The big guy told the waitress of Asian descent in a very loud voice to tell her manager if he had a problem with our service to see him, and if the manager didn't like it, that he would buy the "g d" place and the manager would be the first one fired. Apparently, the manager heard what was said and disappeared. The waitress was obviously taken aback and embarrassed by the comments. I was surprised and saw the big guy face turn red. He did not appear to be joking at all. Later I asked my partner if the big guy was really serious. With a slight smile he said that the big guy wasn't joking, and that was his personality. I had never seen or heard anything like that before or since. Money does talk.

Based on the Mad Men's conversations, I got a firsthand view of how business deals are initiated and made by a handshake. Both men were engaged in a game and enjoying it, while at the same time finalizing what was acceptable or unacceptable in discussing a deal. What an experience for an inner-city Negro who by a strange quirk was sitting at that table at that time and heard that kind of talk. Or was it?

Our last meeting in Philadelphia took place in an old Italian restaurant on the wharf overlooking the Delaware River. It was right out of the movies. I was waiting for gangsters to walk in. The insurance broker, who my colleague and I knew from totally different business situations, arranged for us to meet at this most interesting place. Once we were seated, he introduced us to the owner, we think. He was wearing an expensive double-breasted suit and spoke with an East Coast Italian-style accent, sounding like Sylvester Stallone. He called his nephew (we think) over, saying that he had just arrived from Sicily. The slender young man with slick dark hair could hardly speak English and was obviously nervous. I kept thinking that we were in some kind of gangster movie in which we didn't know we were participants. After all the introductions, the three of us discussed potential clients and possible deals. The Italian food and wine were great. I don't remember if anyone paid for the meals. Leaving the restaurant, I tried to take in what I had just witnessed. What an experience!

# JAMAICA GATHERING

Thanks to a party invitation from a friend in Atlanta, I joined a gathering in Jamaica of Black people from various cities. The opportunity to return to Jamaica came at a good time. Experiencing the sun, sea, sand, and island people began to reenergize me. The Jamaicans, native food, and rum made me feel right at home. And the party was off the hook. There were Black folks from Chicago, Oakland, Detroit, Atlanta, Phoenix, and D.C.; all of whom, men and women, were making their way as entrepreneurs, administrators, and in other endeavors. My stress level went down, which gave way to more positive feelings. What a relief! The worry over money, business concerns, social interactions, and periodic feelings of insecurities began to slip away for the time being.

Given my personal challenges, which are part of life, my business began to grow, which required more of my time. While exhaustion, periodic depression, and demands of my business were ever present, giving up was never an option. My life experiences had prepared me to carry my cross. I remember my great aunt who raised me always said that God never gives anyone more than they can bear. Then there were the difficult, poor, and good decisions that I made along the way. I pray for forgiveness to this day that the poor decisions I made did not adversely affect my fellow human beings. There are valleys in life that we all must travel through in order to reach the other side.

# MARRIAGE LIFE THIRD TIME AROUND

One never knows when or from where blessings will come. On a downtown street I bumped into a person I had known and had not seen in a long time. I had known her sister for quite some time and her mother, both of whom were clients of mine at the time. On one occasion she brought an insurance payment from her sister to my office. She was not happy about the inconvenience of doing so and it showed. We took a tour of the newly renovated office building. After the tour I asked if she would like to meet for lunch and she agreed. We began dating shortly thereafter, trying to feel our way as to how we felt or how close we wanted our relationship to be. She had never been married, and I on the other hand, had been married twice. As time went on, we began to feel that our relationship had potential. Remembering my past marital relationships, I was cautiously determined not to make similar mistakes. Hopeful, I prayed that we were mature, wiser, and better situated for a serious relationship. We appreciated our advantages in that we both enjoyed each other's company, had our own professions, loved travel, liked the same kinds of foods, and had a similar quality of life. I had energy to spare and she was low key. As an observation, opposites attract. After a positive courtship, we decided to marry.

My wife-to-be had the opportunity to attend a national medical meeting in Hawaii. We felt that Hawaii would be a great place to marry as well as honeymoon, and we did so in Kauai. It was an adventure going to Honolulu City Hall, presenting our documentation, filling out necessary papers, and via local friends identifying the kind of Hawaiian minister we wanted. We married in Honolulu outdoors on the beach by a lagoon in front of the Hawaiian Hilton facing Diamond Head with several friends and colleagues present. It was a beautiful, simple wedding. The local Hawaiian minister who conducted the ceremony read from a Hawaiian book of prayer. The words were beautiful as well as powerful and full of meaning. After the wedding our group walked back to our hotel, where we had a small but joyful gathering, something that I will never forget. Although we had a nice reception later back home with family and friends, I was somewhat surprised to hear that some people were curious why we did not marry in a traditional church setting in Indianapolis. We both were happy with our decision to marry in Hawaii. My takeaway from this experience is just be happy, live your life in the now, and enjoy yourself and others. Simple for some to practice yet challenging for many of us. It's all just part of an individual's own journey.

As fate would have it, prior to our wedding, my best man and friend who had traveled from Atlanta and I while walking down the main beach in Honolulu, literally bumped into a former girlfriend of mine. She was there with her husband who was also attending a meeting. Years earlier, she also attended my second wedding in Atlanta. As we looked at each other, it was obvious that we were trying to regain our composure from surprise of such an occurrence. None of us could figure how we could have run into each other so far away from where we lived. My friend just turned to me with a big smile and suggested that we go get a Mai tai.

Different personalities from different backgrounds, my wife and I continue to define who we are as individuals and as a couple. Our experiences as a couple grow through travel, visiting our families and friends wherever they may live, and sharing joy and confidences. We also work at giving each other necessary space to explore our individual interests. The challenges are there and so are the blessings.

It also became clear to me that to be successful in a third marriage I had to have more trust and faith in a higher power. My journey to learn how to trust and develop a true sense of having faith in Mother Father Universe and each other was only in its beginning stages. I discovered that my gift of being a problem solver could also work to my disadvantage. I became aware that I cannot be all things to all people began to slowly make sense. My high expectations of myself and others as well as my sense of adventure and levity were in need of adjustment. However, I strongly believed that my desire to take on challenges, help people through the valleys, and climb mountains have all contributed to my personal growth on earth. As part of my journey, finding the right balance is an everyday happening.

One day as I drove past a yoga center that had recently opened my inner voice directed me to take notice. I had thought about taking up yoga, something that up to that time I had known very little about. The next day I went to the center and without any hesitation signed up to take the class. When asked if I was a beginner and if I had any questions, I asked what time the class started and what I should wear.

Yoga sessions introduced me to a group of people in search of meaning of life and willing to learn about meditation through the practice of yoga/meditation. The yoga instructor was the right person for me, teaching a group of ten. Mimi explained what yoga is and how it can assist us in reaching a better understanding of our physical, mental, and spiritual being. She was very insistent on teaching us the various yoga positions, but it was done in a caring and patient manner. Over a period of time I found that I had more acceptance and patience, and my overall physical wellbeing was improving; I could feel it. I was beginning to feel more confident than before. It was a different kind of self-confidence.

On two separate occasions, my wife and I had opportunities to hear the Dali Lama speak in person. He shared life observations and his wisdom. What a sense of humor! What a blessing to the world! He provided a base for better understanding of oneself and the world. I only had to listen and feel what he was saying. It wasn't complicated. Just feel the love, peace, and joy and work at practicing it wherever one goes. I realized more than before that to become confident in oneself, it takes dedicated practice and discipline. It became apparent that I had to dig deeper within to find my other meaningful self to become more proficient in learning about yoga and life. Yoga was a new pathway. I was placed in a position of teaching myself in understanding the meaning of life and purpose. There was no Annie, grandparents, nuns, mentors, or coaches to encourage me or share their wisdom, in their physical form. It was up to me to interpret external and internal life feedback. The practice of yoga and meditation evolved as an active practice in my life, a beginning, a most welcome beginning.

My wife and I began our marriage journey. As mentioned earlier, we enjoyed visiting our families, especially the grandchildren. Going on picnics, sharing birthdays, Thanksgivings, and Christmases were special treats. My wife's practice was going well and my insurance business was finally beginning to pass the break-even point, yet something was missing in my personal life. I still had a sense of unfulfillment, something I was not doing or did not understand. My internal feelings included anxiety and isolation. As Smokey Robinson has sung, there were tears of a clown. On the outside I had a smile on my face, but when no one was around there were tears of a clown. Why? I also began to notice that periodically I experienced visions and thoughts of things that had not occurred. I just felt that I knew what a person was going to experience or about to say. More often than not, what I had envisioned in the past became a reality or close to it. These kinds of intuitions and premonitions were frightening, and I did not understand them. There were times when talking to a friend or family member that I had to struggle to keep quiet about something that might happen in the future. Yes, there were times that I put my foot in my mouth with much regret. I had to be very mindful when I was asked for advice or listening regarding another's concerns. As time went on I also noticed that friends and some family members would ask for advice or tell me their concerns, waiting to hear what I had to say. Again there were times when I should have kept my mouth shut. Sometimes I saw something and shared my insights. At other times I had to apologize for saying too much. Later in my life, my inner voice put me on notice that there are times I had no right to get into whatever I saw and/or said and that I should apologize or correct what I had previously shared. That was humbling. As more time passed, I responded to inquiries from a point of view of more love and concern with no intent to do harm or predict. If I felt anger, I tried to remain silent or pause and listen to what my inner voice told me to say or how to say it, which worked most of the time. Wisdom does come in time. It all depends on how people see themselves in the world and appreciate that they have something to share. And there are times when people ask about a personal matter that they really don't want to hear. Now I make every effort to be honest, transparent, compassionate, and do no harm.

# SOUTH AFRICA

Early in our relationship, my wife and I realized that we were serious travelers at heart, loved art, and the world was there for us to explore. Thanks to a mutual friend, we had an opportunity to travel to Johannesburg, Cape Town, Pretoria, and Stellenbosch, South Africa, through the People-to-People Ambassador Program. This program provided participants the opportunities for cross-cultural interaction and community service in other countries. Our group's purpose was to visit Black, Indian, and Colored neighborhoods, including being guests in their homes to share dinner and get acquainted. We visited a daycare center, medical facilities, and a major public hospital in Johannesburg. The health care system in the cities were lacking in every sense of the word. It was overwhelmed by the large number of people in need of health care. We also visited the township of Soweto that included its shanty areas where many Blacks were forced to live as a result of apartheid. Nelson Mandela once lived in Soweto. Soweto is also where Blacks began to rise up against the oppressive apartheid and racist South African White government. Many parts of the township suffered from limited access to basic services, if at all. Poverty was visible everywhere. Human beings wherever they may live in this universe should not live under such impoverished or oppressive conditions. Why?

# ITALY

Coming up in a Catholic education system, I had been constantly exposed to the history and teachings of the Roman Catholic Church. With my wife, I was very excited to visit Rome, Florence, Pisa, Siena, and Venice to share in the appreciation of Italy's architecture, art, and history. Coming from the inner city I was not exposed to art and classical music. When I took art and music appreciation class in college, I became curious with the various art forms which had a calming affect on me. In every town we visited we went to museums, churches, and ancient historical sites. Where would human beings be without art and music?

In every Italian city we visited, we walked at every opportunity to be among the people and tried to stay away from tourist groups, especially White Americans. At times we witnessed some ugly Americans acting out their sense of privilege and observed the locals' unappreciative glares.

In Florence, we had the opportunity to visit the gallery that contained the art works of Michelangelo. I was taken back by the size and body details of Michelangelo's *David* statue. What a creation by a human being! My thoughts begin to confirm to me that anything is possible. Creativity is boundless.

There was a funny experience when we were in Venice visiting a small clothing shop patronized by locals. I decided to try on a pair of pants that I still have to this day. The pants were tight around my butt and crotch areas and in need of alteration. The senior sales woman immediately took charge to address the problem. She also asked her assistant to come over to help. With my wife looking on and smiling, one woman was bent over looking and pulling at the material inside and out around my butt and waist and the other woman was on her knees measuring from my crotch area to determine the pants length. Both middle-aged women were communicating in Italian and seemed to pay no attention to our awkward and hilarious position. I had to stand in a frozen position and take it like a man. My wife and I often wondered how it would have looked to another person who walked into the store; and what they would have thought.

While in Venice, my wife and I saw a poster advertising a Mozart opera, *Cosi fan tutte,* featuring the Venice Opera Orchestra at a former sixteenth-century church near the College of Venice. We were given a map, all in Italian, and decided to leave in the late afternoon to find our way and experience the near-by college campus. What a delightful experience listening to Mozart's music and the actors talking and singing in Italian. A new and unforgettable experience for both of us. The opera was over late in the evening. Once we were outside the old church, the reality of the night's darkness made us question what direction to take to get back to our hotel. The small, mostly dark passageways in the neighborhoods were narrow and in places could accommodate only two people side by side, something you don't experience in the United States. There were streetlights attached overhead to buildings, but the dim lights were spaced some distance from each other. At that time of night there were no other neighborhood people on the streets. We experienced the fear of being lost in a strange place late at night without cell phones. Not knowing whether to turn left or right, we walked alone with only our instincts to guide us. There were small canal bridges to cross and no main streets to follow, only small walkways. When we finally reached the Grand Canal area and saw a few landmarks we were familiar with, we were relieved and more confident that we could find our hotel that was located on a side street next to a smaller canal. It took forty-five minutes to reach the hotel, but we made it around midnight.

Again, I struggled to control my fears of being lost in the dark of night. If we had made a wrong turn, we would have been wandering the dark streets of Venice until daylight. Much later I realized that we were guided through the grace of God within us. Now I listen for quiet whispers of guidance and comfort, more confident that my faith in divine guidance will lead me on. The journey is a long one.

In Rome we experienced another interesting episode. One evening my wife and I decided to just walk until we found a place to eat. A nicely dressed Italian man in his fifties who was going in the opposite direction stopped us and asked if he could help us. Surprised and somewhat cautious that someone would walk up to us in the evening and offer anything, we told him that we were just walking as well as looking for a nice place to have dinner. (A footnote: I have had previous adventurous experiences with Gypsies who would suddenly appear and surround a person asking for money, and if people are not on guard, they may have their pocket picked, a common occurrence in Europe.) The Italian gentleman immediately gave us directions of where to go that evening and recommended a nice place to have lunch the next day. He suggested that the outdoor restaurant was a place where people who work in the surrounding area have lunch and that he would stop by, if he could. Were we skeptical? No. His kindness was deeply felt. It was just something about him. I liked his mannerism. To our surprise, he did come by and had lunch. We had a friendly conversation with him as if we have known each other for a long time. After lunch he asked if we wanted to see a fifteenth-century church that many tourists rarely visit. It did occur to me that he wasn't worried about being somewhere in a hurry, nor did he appear to be the hustler type. Being from the inner city, I have seen many slick people trying to sell something or the other. The three of us walked down some very narrow streets into a small neighborhood. There stood the ancient church that reflected the period of when it was built. The outside masonry was dark and gray. If it was a tourist attraction, the outside would have been cleaned up. The inside of the church was dark with paint peeling off, and the centuries-old religious paintings were in poor repair. It seemed like everything was frozen in time, strangely silent and sacred. So much so that we were stunned, trying to comprehend what we were seeing and feeling. It all seemed like we were in an Indiana Jones movie.

We offered to walk our gracious guide back to work, which was not far away. The place of work was a Beverly Hills-type Italian shoe and leather store on the high-end side. Upon entering the store, we noticed the employees all seemed to stop what they were doing and momentarily stare at us, which was strange, like being back in America. I noticed the manner in which our newfound friend was greeted by the salespeople, who were waiting on customers. My wife and I were very impressed with the quality of the leather purses, shoes, and belts and decided to look around. I saw a pair of shoes resembling the kind seen in *GQ* magazine in the States. As we were about to leave and bid our new found friend good-by, we decided to treat ourselves and bring something back from Italy that we would have as a reminder of our time in Italy. We both bought a pair of shoes that we have to this day. The salesperson who waited on me inquired with his Italian accent and smile how we knew Mr. Federico? By that time, it was obvious to us that the distinguished gentleman with the salt and pepper hair was probably the owner of the store. When I told the sales person how we met, he had a quizzical look. A female employee came over and asked if she could do anything else for us. The employees treated us like we were celebrities. Mr. Federico came out of his office and asked what we planned to see and suggested a few places that could be of interest. He then called a person who gave private group tours and asked her to meet us at the small hotel where we were staying.

The woman in a red sport coat came to our hotel. We introduced ourselves. I enjoyed looking at her pleasant quizzical smile, and off we went. During our time with her, we never stood in line to enter the Vatican, museums, or the Coliseum. I kind of felt guilty as we walked past people standing in line. During our time together the tour guide politely asked how we knew Mr. Federico. After we told her how we met, she just smiled.

Before leaving Mr. Federico 's establishment, I had asked for his business card and expressed hope that we would meet again. He indicated that he occasionally visited New York and Las Vegas, but that wasn't the point. I knew that we would never see him again, the soft-spoken elegant man with kindness in his eyes, the man with such self-confidence and coolness. I still think of him from time to time after so many years. The only thing that I could think of in honoring the kindness he shared is to pass it on to others. I think that was the universal purpose.

# SPAIN AND PORTUGAL

Other countries that we liked to visit were Spain and Portugal. The Moor/Islam and Catholic history is on full display with its architecture, art, ancient mosques, Catholic churches, food, and music. The footprint of the African Moors who invaded Spain were everywhere. Their beautiful gardens, tiles, inlays, and open spaces reflected their advanced civilization. The physical makeup of the local people also reflected the diverse nature of the Spaniards. They were friendly and easy to communicate with regardless of the language spoken. They did not appear to be uptight or in a rush, neither did we experience the uncomfortable stares that we often received in the United States of America, land of the free and home of the brave. Casually walking along the narrow streets and the magnificent wide boulevards was a pleasurable experience.

Although we appreciated the gold and silver chalices, crucifixes and other beautiful works of art in the churches and museums, we were very disturbed that much of the gold and silver came from the Americas where Native Americans and African slaves died in order for Spain and Portugal to enjoy their wealth and power. As Portugal and Spain's slavery activities and territories declined, so did their position as a world power.

# ST. PETERSBURG, RUSSIA, AND THE BALTIC COUNTRIES

We had an opportunity to visit several Baltic countries, including Denmark, Finland, Estonia, and Russia. In Denmark and Finland people pay more taxes; however, they seem to live and work in a calmer atmosphere than in the United States. Good healthcare is available for all without the high cost. The statues in the parks have inscriptions acknowledging the rights of mankind. Residents had a live-and-let-live attitude.

We briefly visited Tallinn, Estonia, formerly part of the Soviet republic and next-door neighbor of Russia. The people appeared pleasant, but very wary of Russia.

Our next stop was St. Petersburg, Russia. This beautiful port city on the Baltic Sea is known for its culture and a tumultuous history, in particular the Bolshevik Revolution, the forerunner of the Communist/Socialist Party in Russia. The coming and going through Russian Customs prior to entering and leaving the country was an adventure in itself. The custom officials' stoic expression gave me the feeling that I had stolen something and was about to be caught. My sense of love for humans and curiosity took a back seat to that of caution and fear. I looked in people's eyes and did not detect joy as I understood the definition of joy. I pray that the Russian people find some peace and joy that they deserve as human beings. When our small tour group visited Catherine the

Great's winter palace, known as the Hermitage Museum, my wife and I bumped into three people we knew, two of them were African Americans with whom we had spent some time with in Montreux, Switzerland, two years earlier. We marveled at meeting two African American women we knew in the grand palace, of all places, or was it the Universe just having its way, as is the case with us all?

# RETIREMENT/ GIVING BACK

After ten years in the insurance business, again it was my inner voice that continuously said I should retire and move on. It was time. That feeling began to grow louder throughout my body and mind. There were no pressing reasons why I needed to alter my life's course, but it was time to move on to the next stage of my life, whatever that was.

I was still active at the community level. Our immediate family continued to grow with grandchildren bringing more joy and energy. My wife and I established a scholarship for African American art students at a school of art. After we traveled to other parts of the world, it became very obvious to us that art is an important human expression, and for any society to grow and thrive, education and art are necessary. My wife and I contributed to a new community general hospital in the name of her mother and supported its efforts to more aggressively reach out to the community, especially to the African American community.

What became obvious to us was the more effort we made to extend support to others, the more opportunities we had to do more. The fact that I was blessed to receive a four-year scholarship to attend Cathedral High School where I was provided the opportunity to grow never left my mind or heart. While I was sleeping, my inner voice loud and clear told me that it was time to set up an endowment tuition fund to assist African American students in need of financial assistance to attend Cathedral.

As a person who had to work at a young age and lived on tight budgets, I was fearful in how to take on such a financial commitment. But the reassuring feeling was intense. I stepped out in faith and established an endowed scholarship fund in my name and my family's name for an African American student with financial need. The fund will be available on a continuous basis. Again it was my inner voice that encouraged me to go forward with faith, regardless of any financial limitation. I have faith that this fund will grow over time.

# PHOENIX EXPERIENCE

As part of our five-year plan, my wife and I sold our businesses and moved to Phoenix, Arizona. We periodically visited the City of the Sun and agreed it was a place that we could continue our life journey. We would hike in the mountains and be part of the desert landscape and the diverse nature of the people who live in Arizona. There are Mexican Americans, European Americans, African Americans, Asian Americans, and most importantly, Native Americans scattered throughout the state as well as people from other countries who came to Arizona seeking their place in the sun state. Needless to say there are also those European-American inhabitants who are threatened by that growing diversity. Fortunately human beings do not control the UNIVERSE.

As part of our long-term plan, my wife and I decided to purchase from the proceeds of the sale of our businesses a condominium in Scottsdale, Arizona and rent it out when we were not there. Income from renting the condo paid the monthly mortgage and then some. In the sixth year, we sold the condo and with those proceeds purchased a house in north Phoenix.

Leaving Indianapolis was both an adventure in itself and sad at the same time. To raise money for our move, we sold most of our furniture and began the hard, but fun work of packing. Our family helped with the packing, especially my sister and cousin. Our daughters and their husbands gave us a warm goodbye party, inviting family and close friends. It was more emotional saying goodbye than I thought it would be. Again, I was leaving my daughters, but this time they were their own persons and had good husbands and children. What more could a father ask for? On a bright sunny day in September, my wife and I began our journey to Phoenix. It was an exciting and fun adventure seeing America's diverse landscape, while we were on the road, driving with determined sense of purpose toward our destination. Seeing America on a road trip is highly recommended. Truly God's country. No one owns it, although you may have trouble telling some people that.

Our first night in our Phoenix home was satisfying and a blessing. I have to stop at this point to deeply think about blessings and their meaning to me. Blessing: my wife and I asked for the Universal God's protection and joy during our 1,800-mile trip west. For me it was that inner glow, warmth, and thankfulness of witnessing the glory of God's creation as we traveled and our safe arrival in Phoenix. I believe that we have gone forward not only through planning, but also thanks to the sacrifices and prayers of our concerned family, friends, and ancestors who helped set us on our own course.

In Arizona there are palm, orange, olive trees, cactus, flowers of all types, coyotes, and rattle snakes. The sun does have an effect on the mind and body. We sensed that a heavy burden had been lifted. Having new opportunities in life are a blessing. We understand that we are blessed.

# YOGA, MEDITATION, AWARENESS

It seems like I was destined to take yoga again, and when that opportunity in Phoenix arose, I had no hesitation. The yoga class took place at Unity of Phoenix Church where we attended service. The class consisted of several men and women, Black, Hispanic, and White. Our yoga instructor was a theatrically talented and insightful person. After she left, our group benefitted from another instructor who brought more love. It turned out that it was the right time with the right people and the right space for me. The wisdom of yoga and the practice itself provides a sense of calmness, but more importantly, yoga provides a doorway of becoming aware of how I think, breathe, sleep, and overall familiarity with my body. I became more aware of my conscious self. I remember reading some time ago in *Daily Word*, "Beyond sight, I envision infinite possibilities. Beyond hearing, I listen for quiet whispers of source of guidance. Beyond sensation, I feel harmony with the world around me. I lean in, ready and excited for the next adventure! I breathe in a peace that soothes my emotions, calms my thoughts, and relaxes my body."

When I was entering into the third chapter of life, eternal questions began to rise to the surface. What is my purpose in life? How can I forge a meaningful relationship with my wife, family, and friends? How can I be supportive and a good role model for my daughters, their spouses, and my grandchildren?

I remember writing a note summarizing what the senior minister at Unity Church observed, …. be changed by liberating our minds. Be aware of the stories we are telling ourselves. Stop doing the things that make us unhappy. That in itself will raise our energy and draw good things to us. Being energized to take action will help grow our faith. Say no to the noise inside our heads. Say yes to silence. Say no to our ego that constantly fights to control our minds. It is all about now.

I had questions: How can I personally contribute to the Universe? How can I find a match between my joy and being of service to humankind? What became clear was that I had already placed in my life the practice of yoga and meditation. And it has led me to commitment that deepens my life meaning. The Universe and its blessing and wonders become even more evident. Equally important, I chose to identify with human beings who my intuition encouraged me to trust, listen to and learn from. I am thankful for being directed toward the Light of the World and things seen and unseen. And yes, communicating to the Universal Mother Father God through prayer is clearer and spiritually rewarding. Just listen!

In his book, *Disciplines of the Spirit*, Dr. Thurman explored five major areas for tutoring the human spirit: commitment, growth, suffering, prayer, and reconciliation. Dr. Thurman's teachings and writings helped me in my spiritual search. I have been particularly inspired by his observation, "Don't ask what the world needs. Ask what makes you come alive, and go do it. Because what the world needs is people who have come alive."

Dr. Howard Washington Thurman was an African American educator, poet, theologian, author, mystic, and civil rights leader. Dr. Thurman graduated from Morehouse College. He taught philosophy and religion at Morehouse College, Spellman College, and Howard University. According to a Google description, Dr. Thurman's theology of radical nonviolence influenced and shaped a generation of civil rights activists, and he was a key mentor to leaders within the civil rights movements, including Dr. Martin Luther King, Jr. One of Dr. Thurman's quotes that is impactful to this day is, "During times of war, hatred becomes quite respectable even though it has to masquerade often under the guise of patriotism."

The same is true in the writings of the spiritual mystic and clairvoyant Edgar Cayce resulting in *A Search for God*, Book l and Book ll. In my continued spiritual enlightenment studies, I reread *The Power of Now* by Eckhart Tolle, and the Bible is always nearby. Zen/Buddhist teachings have helped me look inward with more loving kindness for myself.

The calling does not include impressing others as to my good intentions and why I choose to do something for others. It is the joy, the happiness and the self-confidence to be part of mankind's community, just doing from the heart. I wake up to live my purpose each day making better choices.

Many times dreams are the vehicle of informing me where and how I could be of service. I now trust my inner silent voices, my dreams, and follow positive guidance. Although negative dreams come at times, I dismiss them in some way. My acceptance tests are dreams that are based on helping and doing no harm, and they come easily, while fearful/negative dreams fade away, for which I am grateful. Thanks to listening to and personally observing the Dali Lama, Archbishop Desmond Tutu, Nelson Mandela, Depok Chopra, Fannie Lou Hammer, Shirley Chisholm, Colin Powel, Jesse Owens, Miquel Ruiz, Henry Hank Aaron, Linus Pauling, and James Baldwin, I have gained better insight, knowledge, compassion, and, I hope, wisdom. What a blessing that an inner-city African American male would have the honor of personally hearing from wise, intellectual, and spiritually based men and women who have given so much to humankind. I have stopped asking why I was personally exposed to these people with messages of love, sacrifice, and hope. I now understand that it was my journey to learn, listen, and contribute to humankind. It seems that my life's purpose was already laid out before I was born.

I have reflected upon my life's journey up to the present. It is for my own review and to share with family and interested pilgrims. And for them to learn and keep focus on their own precious life, regardless of the ups and downs. Through my ups and downs, I have come to appreciate that love, honesty, faith, trust and friendship are the fruit of the Spirit. Life is about making choices; developing awareness of being in the moment. It's our choice. Do things for the right reasons and pay attention.

## YOGA, MEDITATION, AWARENESS

One day when several things seemed to be going poorly, I came across an affirmation in the *Daily Word*, "My spiritual intuition guides me along a purposeful course. I feel assured by this divine guidance. I call upon all the knowledge I need to make the choices that are mine to make."

As I move in this new direction, doors of opportunity open before me. I walk through those doors with courage, trusting my heart to lead me clearly into the next step of my soul's evolution.

With the guiding Spirit as my compass, I walk with joy appreciating the light that surrounds me. Although I stumble from time to time, my steps are steady, my heart is full, and I move ahead with confidence and resolve. No more questions of What is going on.

At long last I finally understand what Dr. Thurman said long ago: "Whatever God is, he must be love. He must be one with the most completely all-embracing, all-inspiring experience of human life. It is for this reason that, when a man is sure of God, God becomes not only his answer to the deeper needs of life but also sustaining confidence as he moves out upon the highway of life to meet the needs of other men. Wherever such a person goes he is a benediction, breathing peace."

My life's coming and goings provided the opportunity to live many times by trial and error, enjoying life wherever it existed. My lessons learned resulted in understanding that honesty, transparency, and controlling the ego help in realizing one's purpose as to why one exists.

**LOVE, HOPE, COMPASSION**

The following books and articles were used as research and/or inspirations.

Baldwin, James. Nobody Knows My Names. Dial Press 1961

Brown, James & Betty J. Newsom. Album: It's a Man's Man's Man's World, 1966

Buscaglia, Leo. Living, Loving and Learning. N.J. SLACK, Inc.1982

Daily Word. Unity Village, 1901 NW Blue Parkway, Unity Village, Mo

Cayce, Edgar. A Search for God Books I & II. Edgar Cayce Foundation, 1977 and Association for Research and Enlightment, Inc.

Sabir K. Muhammad, forward by Iman P. El-Amin. The Need for Logic in Religion Among African Americans. Designer Communications, 1990

Emerson, Ralph Waldow. Emerson's Essays, Thomas Y. Cromwell, Inc. 1926

Tolle, Eckhart. The Power of Now. Eckhart Tolle, 2004

Thurman, Howard. Discipline of the Spirit, Permission of the Thurman Family.

Jesus and the Disinherited; Beacon Press

Tutu, Desmond & Mpho. Made for Goodness and why this makes all the difference. HarperCollins Publishers

Warren, Rick. The Purpose Driven Life: What on Earth Am I Here For? Zondervan, Publisher

CPSIA information can be obtained
at www.ICGtesting.com
Printed in the USA
BVHW011440011122
650839BV00004B/13